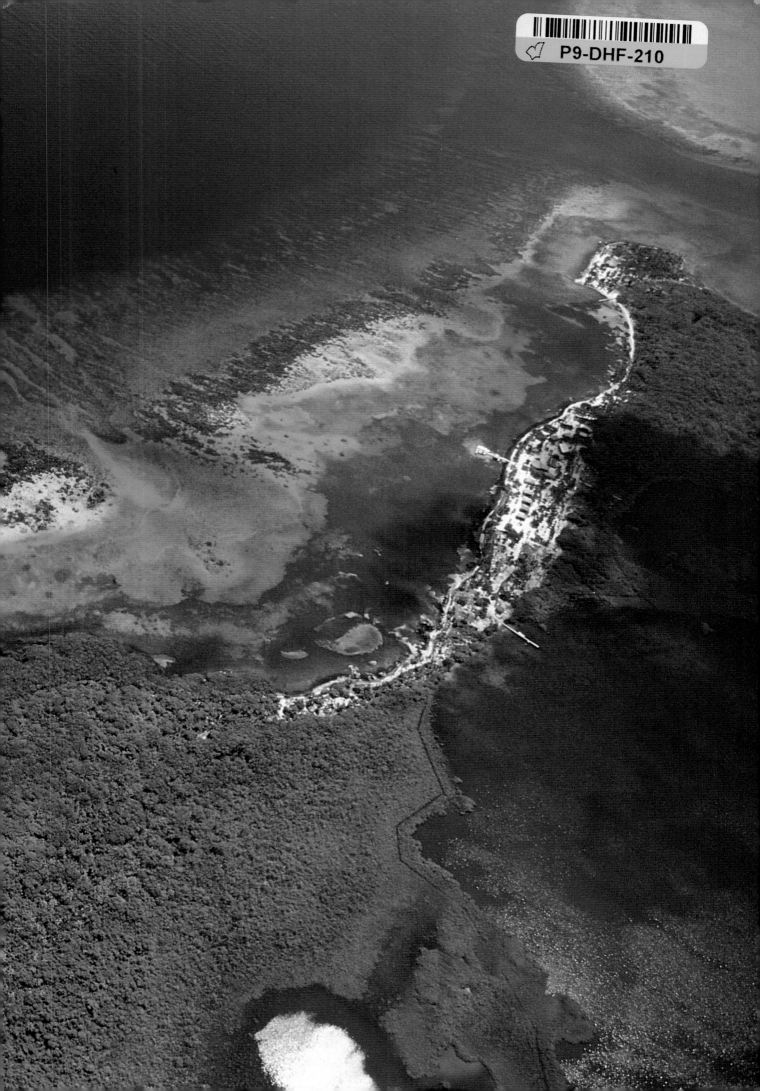

**Text and photographs by Kurt Amsler,
with other contributors:** Daniel Deflorin
(French Antilles); Eleonora De Sabata (Isla de
la Juventud and Cayo Largo); Andrea Ferrari
(Octopus Lair); Angelo Mojetta (Fish of the
Caribbean); John Neuschwander (Dutch
Antilles)

**Illustrators:** Cristina Franco (dive sites),
Monica Falcone (Fish of the Caribbean)

**Translator:** Antony Shugaar

**Copyeditor:** John Kinsella, Diving Science and
Technology Corp.

**Production editors:** Abigail Asher,
Leslie Bockol

**Layout:** Patrizia Balocco, Clara Zanotti

**Text designers:** Barbara Balch, Barbara Sturman
**Jacket designer:** Jordana Abrams

First edition
10 9 8 7 6 5 4 3 2

*Library of Congress Cataloging-in-Publication Data*

Amsler, Kurt.
[Caraibi guida alle immersioni. English]
Diving in the Caribbean / Kurt Amsler.
p.    cm.
Originally published: Caraibi guida alle
immersioni. Vercelli, Italy: Edizioni White
Star, 1996.
Includes index.
ISBN 0-7892-0307-3
1. Deep diving—Caribbean Area—Guide-
books.  2. Scuba diving—Caribbean Area—
Guidebooks.  3. Skin diving—Caribbean
Area—Guidebooks. 4. Caribbean Area—
Guidebooks.  I. Title.
GV838.673.C27A57    1998
797.2'3'09729—dc21
96-52843

# THE CARIBBEAN
## *Dive Guide*

*Text and photographs by*
KURT AMSLER

*Editing provided by*
Diving Science and Technology Corp. (DSAT)
a corporate affiliate of
Professional Association of Diving Instructors (PADI)

ABBEVILLE PRESS PUBLISHERS
*New York   London*

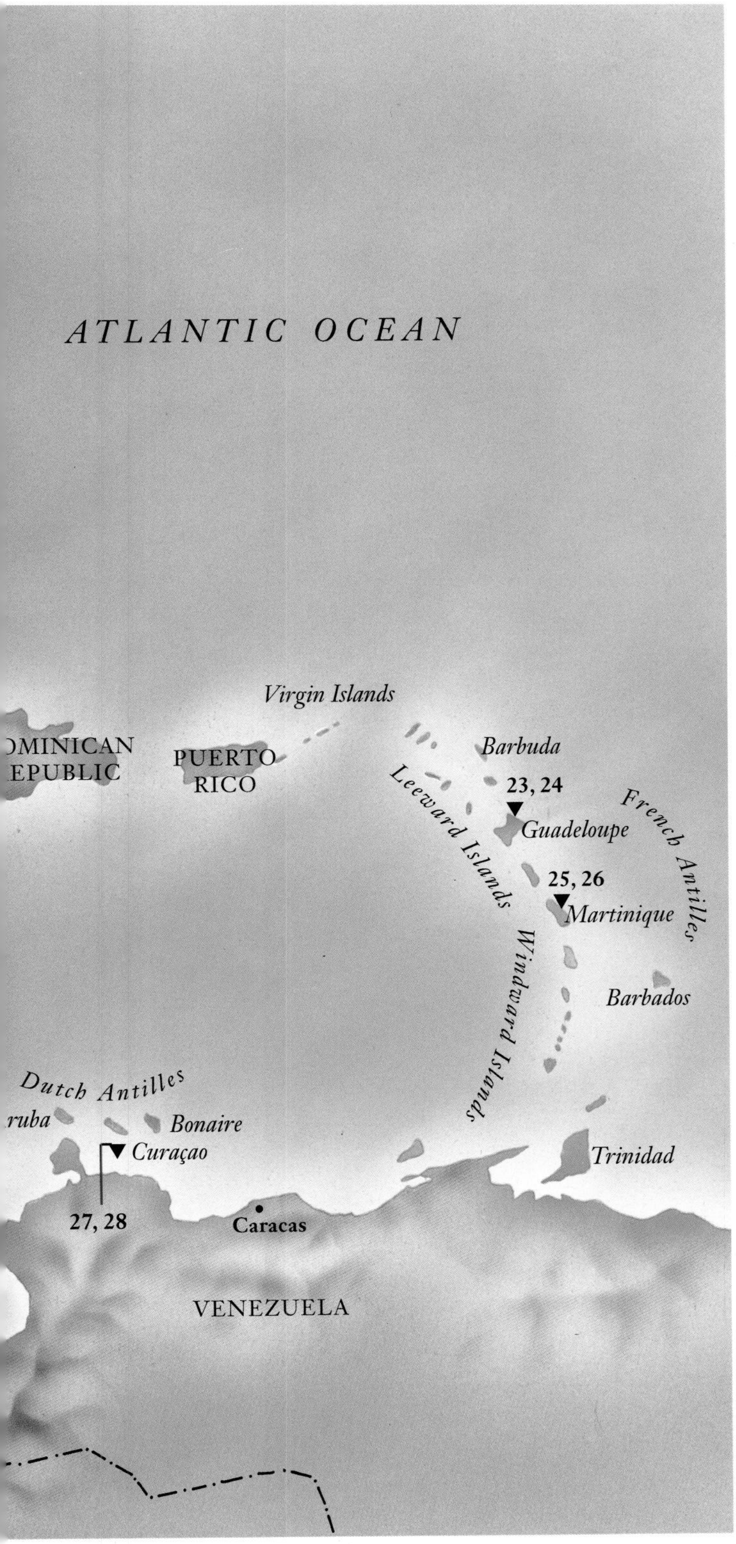

ATLANTIC OCEAN

DOMINICAN
REPUBLIC

PUERTO
RICO

Virgin Islands

Barbuda

Leeward Islands

23, 24

Guadeloupe

French Antilles

25, 26

Martinique

Windward Islands

Barbados

Dutch Antilles

Aruba

Bonaire

Curaçao

Trinidad

27, 28

Caracas

VENEZUELA

*Page 1:*
*The gray angelfish*
*(Pomacanthus*
*arcuatus) is one of the*
*best-known symbols of*
*the Caribbean.*

*Pages 2–3:*
*The incredible colors of*
*the Belize coast.*

# THE CARIBBEAN
## *Dive Guide*

# INTRODUCTION

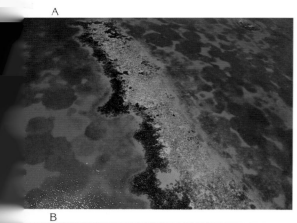

A

*A. Caribbean coral sea beds provide exceptional dive sites, quite different from those of the Indo-Pacific in history and evolution.*

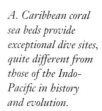

B

*B. Waves and currents continually modify the appearance of the coastline and the underwater reefs. This is the coral reef of Guadeloupe.*

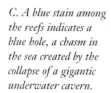

*C. A blue stain among the reefs indicates a blue hole, a chasm in the sea created by the collapse of a gigantic underwater cavern.*

C

D

*D. Thanks to regular rainfall, many Caribbean islands have lush vegetation that often reaches to the edge of the sea.*

European conquerors were the first to call this stretch of the Atlantic "the Caribbean," after the native Caribs. Some maintain that it is the region where Christopher Columbus first set foot in the New World. The Caribbean Sea itself borders Cuba (north), the Antilles (east), Colombia and Venezuela (south), and Central America (west). It is not a coral sea, like the Pacific and the Indian Ocean, and you won't find large coral formations and reefs, but there is nonetheless a sensational underwater world to explore.

The entire western Atlantic offers exceptional subtropical scuba diving. Warm currents keep the water temperature above 68°F (20°C) and encourage the growth of a great variety of unique flora and fauna. The ocean floor, transfigured by violent floods, seismic activity, and volcanic eruptions during and after the Ice Ages, had previously been hundreds of meters higher; it is formed of limestone and lava with innumerable chasms and caves.

Colored sponges of countless shapes are distinctive features of these waters; they grow at all depths reachable by divers and some are large enough to actually get inside. The soft corals and sea fan corals are beautiful—some are very similar to the gorgonians of the Mediterranean. Most of them are found only in this area, growing at depths of 10 to 65 feet (3 to 20 meters). Swimming above them is an enchanting experience. There are some hard corals: huge elkhorn corals, branch corals, yellow fire corals, flat corals, and brain corals. However, it is the sheer walls—called "drop-offs" because they plunge vertically to depths of up to 6,560 feet (2,000 meters)—that shape the most spectacular underwater landscapes and make the most exhilarating dives.

E. Elegant dolphins, jumping and spinning acrobatically in the waves, often accompany dive boats going from one site to another.

F. Big rays are common on sandy floors, especially at Stingray City on Grand Cayman, where they are the main attraction.

The rich variety of living creatures starts with the lower animal species, including snails, bivalves, and worms; these are not much different from corresponding types living in other seas. There are crustaceans of all kinds—crabs, prawns, shrimps, and lobsters—in abundance. Tiny, gaudy reef fish light up the landscape, although their range of colors is narrower than that of tropical fish. Angelfish thrive here—they can measure up to 16 inches (40 centimeters) in length, much bigger than their relations living in other seas. There are gray angelfish, French angelfish, and the splendid gold-and-blue queen angelfish. This is the only place in the world where you will find Nassau groupers. They grow to a considerable size and, in busy dive sites, are as friendly as puppies. Stingrays also find ideal

G. A huge black grouper (Mycteroperca bonaci).

H. To ensure safe diving, sites are often marked with buoys. However, a dive master is in charge of all dives.

A. Large, suspended rock formations found in blue holes are the remains of huge stalactites, which formed when the cave was above sea level.

B. Many of the wrecks scattered over Caribbean sea beds provide popular dive sites. They were often sunk intentionally for the enjoyment of divers.

C. Gorgonians are the predominant organisms on many of the Caribbean reefs. Divers accustomed to the fan-shaped gorgonians typical of other seas are amazed by the variety of shapes found in the Caribbean.

living conditions in these waters—the huge expanses of sandy bottom provide them with a hunting ground rich in crabs and other small animals —and they can grow to a wingspan of more than 3 feet (1 meter). Hundreds of them live in a single Grand Cayman lagoon, which is a great attraction for divers. They are harmless creatures, using the poisonous tip of their tail only in defense. Large fish patrol the drop-offs: manta rays, eagle rays, gray sharks, hammerheads, barracuda, enormous schools of jacks, and (the biggest of them all) the whale shark.

From the Florida Keys to the southernmost Antilles, sport diving is professionally organized. All the islands and coasts open to tourism have efficiently equipped dive bases that work on American standards, providing modern equipment and a guarantee of safety. The best diving

B

C

A

D

D. In addition to gorgonians and corals, sponges are a classic element of America's tropical Atlantic coastline.

E

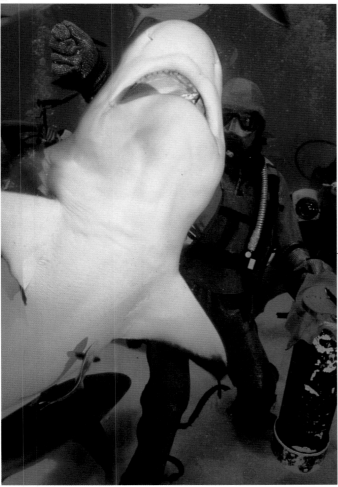

F

G

H

F. Life on the sea bottom provides continual inspiration for enthusiastic underwater photographers.

G. A spotted goatfish (Pseudopeneus maculatus).

H. A striking palette of colors can be found amidst the wealth and variety of Caribbean sea life.

E. It is not uncommon to meet sharks in the Caribbean. In some places, such as Shark Junction in the Bahamas, divers can watch sharks being fed.

areas include (from north to south) the Florida Keys, the Bahamas, the Yucatan (Cozumel, Cuba, Turks and Caicos), the Cayman Islands, Belize, Honduras (Guanaja), the Virgin Islands, the French Antilles, and the Dutch Antilles. The allure of the Caribbean archipelago—great weather, beautiful underwater landscape, and well-equipped resort facilities—is only enhanced by its people. Their optimistic outlook, reflected in their music, is a relief to stress-worn tourists. They will regale you with thrilling stories of treasure hunters and mutinies over a drink in one of the many "Buccaneers' Taverns" or "Pirates' Pubs." Afterward, you may even see a foggy image of the infamous Henry Morgan himself on the dock at midnight. . . .

# Underwater Photography

A

B

C

*A. A photographer focuses in on a pair of angelfish.*

*B. The great variety of marine organisms makes for great photographs.*

*C. The fascinating world of macro-photography: a close-up view of a toadfish (Batrachoides gilbertis).*

*D. Big yellow sponges and colonies of sea-plume gorgonians are favorite subjects for photographers in Caribbean waters.*

*E. There are many splendid subjects for photographers at all depths: on the sea floor, throughout the reef, and around the fascinating wrecks.*

D

E

Many scuba divers find that underwater photography adds a new dimension to the sport. With a camera in hand, you pay closer attention to everything, understand animal behavior better, and generally have a more intense diving experience. The photographs also let you relive your dives with friends at home. Some divers have become excellent underwater photographers; others would like to start but lack confidence in their ability to take high-quality, colorful pictures. Such pictures may have been elusive several years ago, but today the market offers modern, easy-to-use underwater cameras that almost guarantee good pictures. The most popular are Motormarine and Nikonos, which are totally waterproof. Special underwater housings are also available for traditional automatic cameras. It is a good idea to take an underwater photography course, available in diving schools all over the world, to learn some of the basic skills.

The diverse underwater world of the Caribbean, with its splendidly colored coral and fish, offers some great opportunities for photography. The topography of the sea bed and the lie of the reef provide wonderful subjects in waters as shallow as 16 to 98 feet (5 to 30 meters). At these depths there is excellent sunlight, which plays a very important role in getting sharp images and good color; still, a flash will give you better colors and an even deeper blue background. A flashgun is certainly fundamental to wide-angle shots. Another important element in getting a good image is the transparency of the water. Each area of the Caribbean has a specific season of poor, but not impossible, visibility, but you can almost always count on virtually ideal conditions for photography. Thanks to the bright, transparent water, you don't need special film; the best results are obtained with 100 ASA/ISO.

You will definitely want to bring your camera on one of the wreck dives described in this book. To get the best shots, use a wide-angle lens, specifically 14 to 20 millimeters. With a normal lens, you have to move too far away from the subject to frame it. Wide-angle, or fish-eye, lenses also deliver greater depth of field over the entire photograph. For smaller subjects (gorgonians, soft corals, tubular and barrel sponges,

*F. The water's clarity is an important factor in taking good photographs.*

and small fish), the ideal focal width is from 20 to 28 millimeters. Keep a distance of between 2.5 and 5 feet (1 and 1.5 meters) to get the most precise images, best contrast, and truest colors.

Tiny invertebrate species (vividly colored sea worms, slugs, prawns, and crabs) live close to, above, and inside coral. Details of soft corals, anemones, sponges, and blennies make perfect macro-photography (close-up) subjects. For close-ups of individual subjects (fish, anemones, and small sponges and gorgonians) use 35- to 50-millimeter lenses and select an aperture between f8 and f11 to reduce focal distance to less than 3 feet (1 meter). Lighting such small subjects is easy with the right accessories. Use superimposed lenses, intermediate rings, or special macro lenses, depending on your camera. A TTL flash gun guarantees perfect lighting.

Camera equipment used in the salt water of the tropics needs a lot of care. Immediately after the dive, immerse the camera in fresh water for ten minutes; this is the only way to eliminate the sand particles and salt crystals from the O rings and apertures. To make sure that the camera and the flash remain absolutely watertight, check the O ring at every change of film. Clean the O ring of any deposits by running it gently through your finger and thumb; check for any damage at the same time. Clean the O-ring channel with a paper tissue. Black neoprene O rings must not be over-greased, but grease the orange silicone ones well to provide an efficient seal. At the end of a vacation trip, immerse all photographic equipment in a solution of fresh water and vinegar (about 1 teaspoon of vinegar to 1 quart [1 liter] of water) for half an hour; this removes all saline corro-

*G, H. On night dives, strange creatures appear on the sea bottom: a giant basket star (Astrophyton muricatus), top, and an evanescent tuft on a coral branch.*

G

H

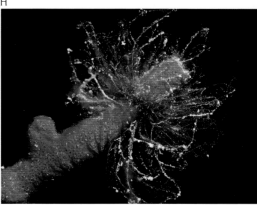

sives from metallic components. Rinse everything for a further hour in fresh water and dry carefully. Grease the O rings, or remove them if you do not expect to use the camera for a long time. While traveling and especially on the dive boat, it is best to carry your equipment in a rigid padded plastic case. Don't forget to bring enough film, spare batteries, spare O rings, and everything you need for maintenance.

# Grand Bahama

**G**rand Bahama is among the most northerly of the 700 islands and 2,500 cays in the Bahamas archipelago, which stretches south 60 miles (95 kilometers) east of the Florida coast all the way to Cuba. The islands used to be peaks of a plateau 330 feet (100 meters) above sea level during the Ice Age.

When the ice melted, the water level rose and almost submerged the plateau, leaving the peaks as islands and turning the lower ground into underwater reefs, now rich in corals and fish of every kind. The highest point in the Bahamas today is the 215-foot (65-meter) peak on Cat Island.

The island scenery itself is not very interesting, but even with only a mask and fins you can explore beautiful shallow reefs just off the coast. The sea bed, covered with soft corals, slopes down to the medium reefs, then to the deep reefs, and finally to the drop-offs.

Some maintain that when Columbus reached the New World in 1492 he first landed on the Bahamas. Spanish navigator Ponce de Leon was the first European to explore the island of Grand Bahama. But Spain considered it (like many other islands) lacking in any exploitable resources, and it was the English who eventually colonized it. The islands' economy ran on fishing and sponge-fishing— and, during Prohibition in the United States, rum smuggling, so piracy prevailed for many years. Everything changed in the 1950s, when American financiers negotiated a historic agreement with the English to promote tourism in the area in exchange for enormous tax concessions. The agreement continued even after the Bahamas became independent in 1973.

GRAND BAHAMA

GREAT ABACO

ELEUTHERA

NEW PROVIDENCE

**Nassau**

ANDROS

CAT

LONG ISLAND

CROOKED ISLAND

ACKLINS    MAYAGUANA

GREAT INAGUA

A

B

*A. This sponge features treelike branches.*

*B. The light of the flashgun clearly shows the color of this longspine squirrelfish (Holocentrus rufus). The fish was caught out in the open, next to the unusual branches of a candlestick gorgonian with large polyps.*

Grand Bahama Island is 70 miles (113 kilometers) long by 8 miles (13 kilometers) wide. The form of its reef is typical of the area: shallow reef, medium reef, deep reef, and drop-off (known as "the edge of the ledge"). The most interesting reef is along the south coast, where, less than a mile offshore, the reef descends rapidly into the New Providence Channel. At the East End, the shallow Little Bahama Bank separates Grand Bahama from the Abaco Islands. The coral bank is famous among divers for its wild spotted dolphins.

There are excellent provisions for all diving sports organized under the auspices of UNEXSO (the Underwater Explorer Society). Fifty-seven permanent buoys mark the areas reserved for diving, which, because of their distance from the coast, can only be reached by boat. Most sites are between Silver Point to the west and Lucayan Waterways to the east. They can all be reached by boat in relatively short times, varying from 15 minutes to 1 hour, starting from the UNEXSO base. The farther, less popular sites on the coral reef (such as Deadman's Reef or East End) require full-day trips.

Thanks to the Gulf Stream, the temperature of the water never falls below 68°F (20°C), and it rises as high as 85°F (28°C) from May to September. There are no particularly strong currents in the most popular dive sites, although divers should watch for medium-strength currents, depending on the wind, the waves, and the tides; use the dive entry and exit buoys.

Many water-filled craters (sinkholes) can be found inland, and you can investigate enormous caves full of stalactites and long, labyrinthine tunnel complexes. There is a splendid grotto, called Ben's Cave after its discoverer, Ben Rose. All diving in this sinkhole is regulated and organized by UNEXSO.

The underwater world of Grand Bahama is typical of the Caribbean, with two spectacular attractions that attract divers from all over the world: Shark Junction and the Dolphin Experience. UNEXSO is behind the introduction of scuba diving with Caribbean reef sharks and bottlenose dolphins.

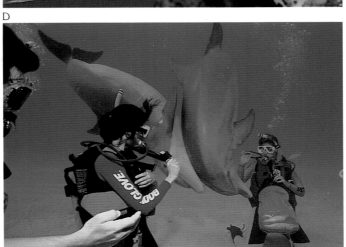

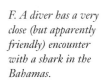

C. The peculiar body coloring of a black grouper (Mycteroperca bonaci) can be seen in this close-up.

D. Dolphins playing with scuba divers in Grand Bahama.

E. This curious coral formation (Dendrogyra cylindrus) looks almost like a modern sculpture.

F. A diver has a very close (but apparently friendly) encounter with a shark in the Bahamas.

# Grand Bahama: Shark Junction

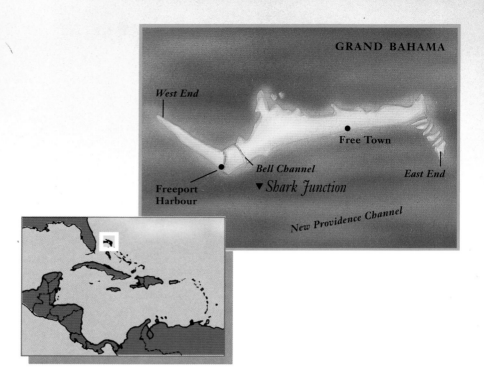

GRAND BAHAMA

West End

Free Town

Bell Channel

Freeport Harbour

East End

▼ Shark Junction

New Providence Channel

0 m
0 ft

16 m
53 ft

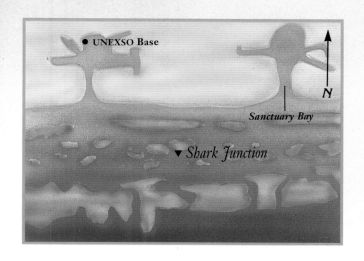

UNEXSO Base

Sanctuary Bay

▼ Shark Junction

N

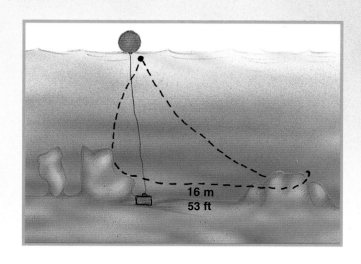

16 m
53 ft

## LOCATION

*A. Every dive at Shark Junction is preceded by a detailed briefing in the UNEXSO seminar rooms to explain the different stages of the dive.*

*B. The shark carousel starts almost as soon as you reach the sea bottom.*

An encounter with a shark is an unforgettable experience for divers. Their timidity can be a problem, especially for photographers, who usually can't get close enough to get a good look. At Shark Junction there are twenty Caribbean reef sharks *(Carcharhinus perezi)* with which you can swim. There are permanent buoys for descent and resurfacing just over a mile from

Bell Channel. The dive masters feed the sharks in a sandy circular clearing on the sea bed 50 feet (15 meters) deep, close to the medium reef. You will also see enormous moray eels, who live among the corals surrounding the arena, big southern stingrays, and more than 10 huge groupers who visit regularly. Swim into the open sea to see large banks of jacks crossing and get the full effect of the sharks' silhouettes against the deep blue.

A

D

B

C

## THE DIVE

The adventure begins with a detailed briefing at the UNEXSO base, during which your dive master runs through the various phases of the dive. Although the sharks at this site have become used to these encounters over the years, divers have to stick rigorously to the established procedure to guarantee the group's safety.

The journey to Shark Junction only takes half an hour. The 20 jacks used to bait the sharks are stowed in a special container at the dock. The dive master wears a stainless steel mesh ("chain mail") suit to facilitate his control over the sharks. The sharks never bite without reason, but sometimes two will go for the same bait, grazing the feeder's hand in passing with their razor-sharp teeth. There are also two security guards

*C. Sharks and divers come face to face at the sea bottom, perhaps with mutual feelings of curiosity and fear.*

*D. The Caribbean reef sharks* (Carcharhinus perezi) *often bump into each other in their haste to tear a fish from the hands of the instructor.*

*E. The final instants of a shark's approach are always thrilling. Note the chain mail— a recognition of the potential danger.*

*F. Other fish often join in to eat scraps left by the sharks. Here are some yellowtail snappers (Ocyurus chrysurus).*

E

F

and the camera man present. The security men accompany the group to the arena, where there is an inoperative decompression chamber in front of which the divers kneel in a semicircle. You will see the sharks circling even before you reach the arena. Some come within a few meters of the group and swim calmly among the divers. They are all females, varying in length from 5 to 6.5 feet (1.5 to 2 meters). Dark mottled groupers will start to arrive from all directions, southern stingrays settle in the sand, and the water is alive with yellowtails. As if obeying a command, all the creatures will suddenly start to swim in the same direction—toward the dive master with the food container. Weighed down by the metal suit and with fins off, he moves along the sand to the sandy clearing, followed by a horde of sharks. Just 6.5 feet (2 meters) from the divers, the first fish is offered to the sharks, who become animated, swimming in ever tighter circles around the dive master. Their movements are calm and controlled, though they are not tense. You have to watch carefully to see the shark raise its nose, thrust its jaw forward, and close the nictitating membrane over its eyes—it all happens in a few seconds. The dive master will do his best to ensure that you get a good look and the cameraman will videotape the whole dive for you as a souvenir (so you don't have to bring your own camera).

After about twenty minutes, more sharks arrive, moving so quickly that they are difficult to count. When the sharks feel the supply of jacks running out, they close in on the dive master, who is actually able to embrace and stroke them. The dive master then draws the group of sharks out of the arena with the last of the bait.

These encounters are more significant than you might think. One hundred million sharks are exterminated as predators and enemies to humans each year. The experiences people have at Shark Junction or at similar exhibitions may help end mankind's unreasonable fear of sharks and save these precious creatures from extinction.

G
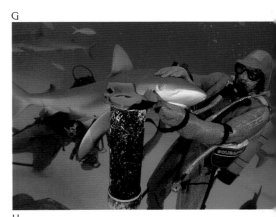

H

*G. Some female sharks, which can measure over 6.5 feet (2 meters) long, will let dive masters embrace and stroke them.*

*H. At the end of the feeding, the sharks disperse, but never too far from the center of their territory.*

# *Grand Bahama:*
# Theo's Wreck

GRAND BAHAMA

*West End*

Free Town

Silver Point

Xanadu Beach

Freeport
Harbour

▼ *Theo's Wreck*

*East End*

0 m
0 ft

27 m
90 ft

33 m
108 ft

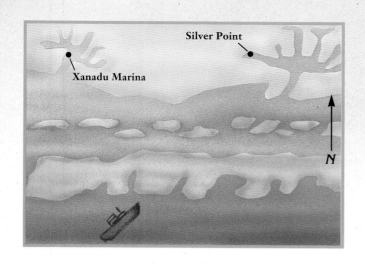

Xanadu Marina

Silver Point

N

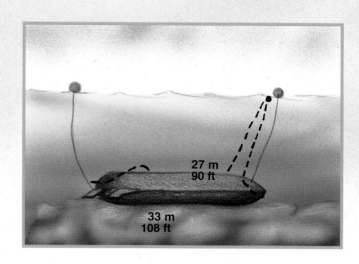

27 m
90 ft

33 m
108 ft

## LOCATION

This dive site is west of Bell Channel, between Silver Point and Xanadu Beach, about 1.5 miles (2.5 kilometers) from the coast. The wreck is about 230 feet (70 meters) long and rests on the ocean floor on its port side, between the deep reef and the drop-off at a depth of about 108 feet (33 meters). The bow points landward and the stern seaward. The rudder and propeller hung over the edge of the ledge until hurricane Andrew moved the wreck a few meters closer to shore. It rests on a

A. The ship's prow, with its anchor chain still in place, lies at a depth of around 108 feet (33 meters) and appears to be slightly raised off the ground.

B. All the machinery on the bridge is still intact, but it has been transformed by incrustations into lively blotches of color that are revealed only by artificial light.

C. The water here is so transparent that almost the whole outline of the wreck can be seen, even from a distance.

D. The number of visiting divers attests to the fascination of Theo's Wreck, now one of the most popular dive sites in the Bahamas.

flat, sandy floor, among a few isolated coral banks. Two permanent marker buoys, one at the prow and one at the stern, mark the ship's position. The waters around the wreck are subject to currents that vary according to the wind, waves, and tides; use the buoys for safe resurfacing.

Since it sank in 1982, the ship has become home to numerous fish and is now covered with rich vegetation. The bow anchor chain, in particular, has splendid gorgonian sea fans. The shaded part of the hull is completely smothered in orange false gorgonians.

## THE SHIP'S HISTORY

Built in Norway in 1954, the *M/S Logna* was used to carry cargo between Norway and Spain. The Bahama Cement Company acquired it in 1969 to take sand from Fort Pierce, Florida, to Eleuthera and

New Providence (Nassau). A million dollars was allocated for restructuring the ship so that it could be registered with Lloyd's in 1981. However, the investment could not be amortized and the ship was decommissioned at the Bahama Cement Company dock. When the management decided to scuttle the ship in deep international waters, engineer Theopolis Galanoupoulos, an underwater sports enthusiast, suggested sinking it in shallower water as an attraction for scuba divers. UNEXSO helped to get the necessary authorization, the ship was towed to the designated spot, and the valves in the ballast tanks were opened on October 16, 1982. However, barnacles blocked the pipes and the scuttling lasted for hours. The delay put the ship at risk of being lost because strengthening winds pushed it ever closer to the drop-off. Tension reached indescribable levels with only minutes to spare—but fortunately the *M/S Logna*, known ever since as *Theo's Wreck*, sank in time.

## THE DIVE

We moor our boat to the buoy at the bow of the ship. A glance over the parapet reveals a light current, and the blue of the water is a guarantee of excellent visibility. The briefing is an important part of the dive and is done in detail by the instructors. We start the dive along a cable that leads from the boat platform to the mooring buoy and eventually to the wreck. Visibility is exceptional. We can see the outline of the boat clearly from the surface of the water and, looking over the parapet, I see a huge shoal of jacks and numerous barracuda. We enter at the bow, where the anchor chain hangs down, covered with splendid gorgonians. The strobe light being used to make the film of the dive shows the corals in all the splendor of their true colors. Close to the bow of the wreck, the depth is 108 feet (33 meters). The exploration starts on the bow deck and we move on to the first cargo hold. An enormous shoal of grunts almost blocks the way and, totally ignoring the divers, disappears inside the ship. We swim to the superstructure at the center of the huge holds. With a torch, I can see the numerous animals hiding in the nooks and crannies. Two enormous green moray eels live here in all but the summer months. The shoal of grunts has collected in front of us, almost as if they would like to be our guides, and they move as we pass by, revealing the superstructures. There is a lot of life down here. Many fish hide among the struts, the braces, and the ventilation pipes, and the shoal of jacks is still swimming around the deck and the

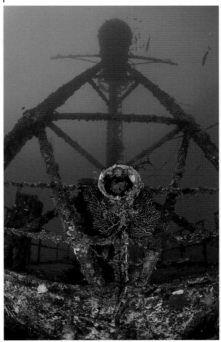

toppled chimney. It is incredible how, in just a few years underwater, the ship has been covered in vegetation. The winches on the quarter-deck are beautiful. We intend to get as far as the propellers and the rudder so we leave the quarter-deck and head for the starboard parapet. There we feel the presence of the light current from which we were sheltered on the other side of the ship and inside the holds. The underside of the rudder and the enormous curved propeller blades are com-

pletely covered with flower corals in wonderful shades of orange. We see a long line of big lobsters at the point where the hull disappears into the sand, just a few yards away from the stark outline of the drop-off. Sharks, rays, and sea turtles come in at this point from the open sea to visit the wreck. Other divers told me of a 15-minute encounter they had with a school of spotted dolphins just a few days before I arrived on Grand Bahama. Swimming toward the bow, we are sheltered from the current by the deck and are able to admire *Theo's Wreck* in perfect tranquillity.

*E. Many fish find refuge inside the huge holds of* Theo's Wreck.

*F. The bridge scaffolding was quickly covered by huge deepwater gorgonians, sponges, and corals.*

*G. The winches on the bridge are still recognizable, even though they are almost completely encrusted with organisms.*

*H. The huge propeller blades on the bottom mark the deepest part of the dive. The dropoff starts near here.*

# Grand Bahama:
# The Dolphin Experience

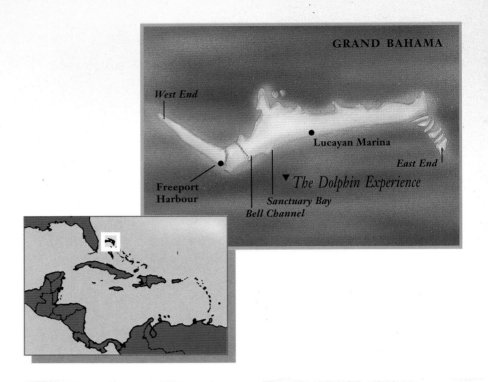

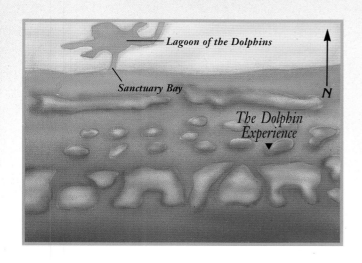

Lagoon of the Dolphins

Sanctuary Bay

The Dolphin Experience

N

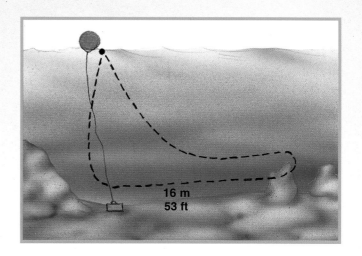

16 m
53 ft

0 m
0 ft

16 m
53 ft

## LOCATION

Very few underwater experiences can compare to a dive in which you've witnessed the beauty, grace, and energy of dolphins. On Grand Bahama, divers can usually expect to be followed by dolphins out into the open sea. The Dolphin Experience was Mike Schulz's idea. He decided to give up his job as a dolphin trainer and release the dolphins imprisoned in tanks into a better environment. The animals released from the dolphinaria underwent months of training before facing the open sea. They live now in a lagoon called Sanctuary Bay to the east of Lucayan Marina, in quiet, deep, protected waters kept clean by the tides. The group usually consists of 6 bottlenose dolphins (*Tursiops truncatus*). Dolphins are intelligent, and these have come to know and love this place.

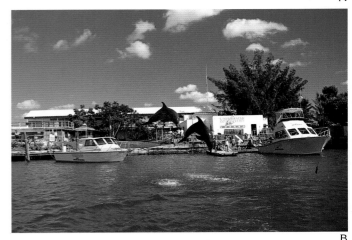

A

B

C

D

The meeting point is on the medium reef at a depth of 50 feet (15 meters), on an almost flat sandy clearing where there are big coral banks. The relatively shallow depth and the reflection of the sun on the sandy bottom make this stretch of barrier reef among the best for photography. The boat usually sets out from the UNEXSO base and divers are briefed during the trip to Sanctuary Bay. All divers must know how to behave in the presence of the dolphins and learn the signals to which the dolphins respond.

Leaving Sanctuary Bay, the dolphins follow our boat and the backup boat toward open sea. Not all the dolphins are interested in humans, and they are never forced to interact. Sometimes this group meets other dolphins of the same species and can disappear for days before returning to Sanctuary Bay.

*A. The UNEXSO base is the starting point for dives with the dolphins.*

*B. Dolphins take part in the compulsory predive briefing during a trip to Sanctuary Bay.*

*C. Interaction with the dolphins can begin the moment the divers start readying the boat.*

*D. Dolphins never fail to emerge to greet their visitors. They have learned to interpret many signals from the humans.*

*E. The dolphins will let all divers touch them gently and calmly.*

*F. The dolphins are completely free in these calm, sheltered waters. It is their own decision whether or not to approach a diver.*

*G. All divers find that such close contact with dolphins is unforgettable.*

*H. The feeding session marks the end of each dive, and reinforces the bond between the instructor and the dolphins.*

## THE DIVE

Keep a camera, fitted with a light telephoto lens, handy during the journey to the dolphin reef; the dolphins that do follow the boat perform incredible acrobatics in and out of the bow waves. You can judge quite easily at what point they will leap out of the water and get some wonderful shots.

We descend 50 feet (15 meters) to the sandy bed, where we arrange ourselves in a circle. Four dolphins appear immediately. They swim around us at high speed, rushing to the surface and then plunging back into the depths, as if they were demonstrating their strength and skill. Their hydrodynamic bodies flying through the water make a fantastic sight and it occurs to me that they really enjoy themselves here. When the instructor goes deeper, taking the bag of food with him, the group calms down, as if they realize that the moment has come to do something for the guests. There is one strictly enforced rule with the dolphins: No work, no food.

The program changes each time; divers can either hitch a ride with the dolphins or feed them. The important thing is to remember the signals from your briefing, otherwise you run the risk of being completely ignored by the dolphins. It is particularly interesting to watch them go to the surface to breathe. Every movement they make is infinitely calm, which makes for great photographs and videos. Not all their games involve the divers, so find a comfortable spot for yourself in their habitat and watch them closely.

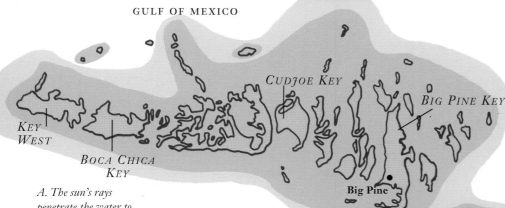

GULF OF MEXICO

*Cudjoe Key*

*Big Pine Key*

KEY WEST

*Boca Chica Key*

Big Pine

ATLANTIC OCEAN

*Boot Key*

Marathon

*A. The sun's rays penetrate the water to illuminate the rich undersea world of Key Largo, Florida.*

*B. A diver's torch lets us admire the rich colors of the underwater fauna: gorgonians, sponges, and corals.*

A

B

There are those who say that Christopher Columbus was the first European to discover the land we know today as Florida. Others say that Spain had first claim, thanks to the boredom of Juan Ponce de Leon. Finding life in the colony of San Juan (now Puerto Rico) too tranquil and monotonous while he was governor, Ponce de Leon decided to abandon his position and dedicate himself to adventuring. He obtained an agreement with the Spanish crown in 1512 that allowed him to explore and colonize new lands. Local legends told of wide beaches to the northwest of the Bahamas, so he took this as his first direction. In 1513 he sailed from the Bahamas, and at Easter-time did indeed reach those legendary beaches. Easter is the festival of flowers (*flores*) in Spain, so he called the place "La Florida." The expedition headed south along the coast and the Florida Keys, which the crew named *Los Martires* ("terror" or "fright"). Many ships traveling this area, including the famous Spanish silver fleet the Tierra Firma, were wrecked by hurricanes that forced them onto the reef. To salvage the treasure that had disappeared into the water, the Spaniards used diving experts—pearl fishermen from the island of Margarite in Venezuela, who could dive to depths of up to 98 feet (30 meters) using heavy stones as ballast. With their help, the Spaniards recovered most of the lost treasure.

## GEOGRAPHICAL POSITION

The Florida Keys form an archipelago of more than two hundred islands that are basically an extension of the Florida peninsula. They stretch from northeast to southwest for over 130 miles (212 kilometers). The subtropical vegetation and the warm climate are the result of the islands' position along the Florida Bank, which channels in the warm water of the Gulf Stream. Thirty-four of the islands are linked by 42 bridges that form the famous highway US 1, 115 miles of road marked off with mile markers, essential to finding your way around the Keys. Key Largo is at mile marker number 100.

## DIVING IN THE KEYS

The coral reefs are much farther from the coast here than in the Bahamas. The width of the Florida Bank varies between 4 and 7 miles (7 and 11 kilometers) and is divided into several zones. The coastal zone is a shallow sea bed with mangroves and zosteras. It is the breeding and

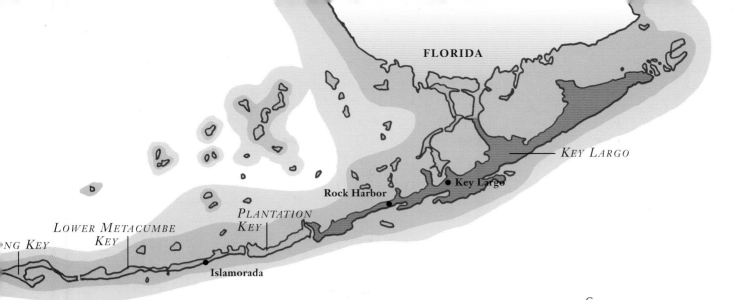

FLORIDA

KEY LARGO

Rock Harbor

Key Largo

PLANTATION
KEY

LOWER METACUMBE
KEY

NG KEY

Islamorada

rearing ground for many marine species, and so is of enormous ecological importance. The midchannel reef is made up of single coral banks, often surrounded by zosteras. At this point, the sea bed is slightly deeper, although it is rarely more than 10 to 16 feet (3 to 5 meters). Coral banks make up the offshore zone, too, but here they grow almost to the surface. In this section of the reef, there are many buoys and light towers to mark the shallows. This is the part of the Florida Bank where visibility is at its best and the most interesting dive sites begin. The sea bed slopes gently to the deep reef, where the corals create deep canyons, grottoes, and long "fingers" along the sands. Out in the open sea, where the coral barrier gives way to a wide sandy bed, depths vary between 55 and 65 feet (17 and 20 meters). Because the reef extends so far from shore, all underwater activities require dive boats. You can hire these boats privately, or join an excursion at one of the numerous dive centers. As everywhere else, divers have to show a dive certificate. All the boats on the Keys are designed especially for diving and have to be U.S. Coast Guard–approved. Everything is approached very professionally and onboard safety has absolute priority. You can get detailed information about every

C

D

C. A grouper peers out curiously from the delicate branches of a sea plume.

D. Two elegant gray angelfish swim close to the sandy bottom.

site and opt for group dives unaccompanied by an instructor.

The flora and fauna are typically Caribbean and protected by the marine sanctuary around Key Largo. All types of coral and a multitude of species of fish thrive here. This underwater park, the first in the United States, was set up in 1960 and bears the name John D. Pennecamp. Pennecamp was a journalist with the *Miami Herald* who was

active in the local battle to protect the region's nature. In 1990 the park was enlarged when a further 2,600 square nautical miles were declared protected. The environment comes first here and severe regulations are applied. The area is 25 miles (39 kilometers) long and 9 miles (15 kilometers) wide, stretching over 3 miles (5.5 kilometers) into the sea to depths of 295 feet (90 meters).

# Key Largo: *The* Duane

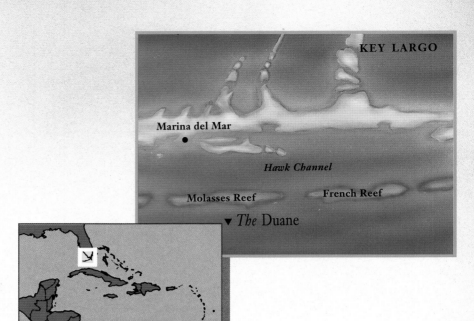

KEY LARGO

Marina del Mar

Hawk Channel

Molasses Reef          French Reef

▼ *The* Duane

0 m
0 ft

15 m
50 ft

27 m
90 ft

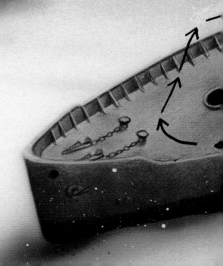

33 m / 108 ft

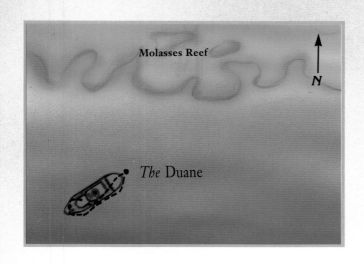

Molasses Reef

N

*The* Duane

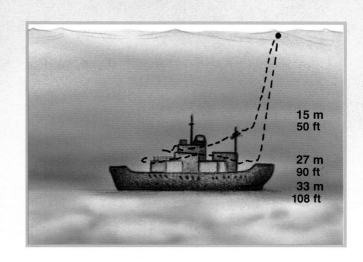

15 m
50 ft

27 m
90 ft
33 m
108 ft

## LOCATION

The wreck of the *Duane* is on a large sandy sea bed scattered with small coral formations at a depth of 108 feet (33 meters), about a mile (less than 2 kilometers) off the south coast of Molasses Reef. A large yellow buoy marks its position and there are 2 dive boat moorings below the surface of the water.

## THE STORY OF THE *DUANE*

This U.S. Coast Guard vessel was commissioned in 1936 and named after the American secretary of the treasury, William J. Duane. Initially, she plied the route linking Oakland, California (her port of registry), with the Alaskan coast. Ship and crew were put to the test in 1939 when the vessel was transferred to wartime service. On their first north-Atlantic patrol, they saved the crew of a torpedoed British steamship. The *Duane* was armed when the United States became actively involved in the war, and in 1943 the crew

attacked a German submarine. It used depth charges to force the sub to surface, and employed cannon fire to sink it; 20 survivors were handed over to British authorities. The crew of the *Duane* distinguished itself again in the Mediterranean when it rescued 250 survivors after the tragic sinking of the troop carrier *Dorchester*. On August 15, 1944, the ship took part in the Allied invasion of southern France. At the end of the war she was once again refitted, this time as an aircraft carrier, and commissioned in the Atlantic. She played guardian angel once more and rescued the

A

27 crew members of Finnish merchant vessel *Bornholm*, which went down in the middle of the ocean on May 4, 1957. In December 1967, she was assigned to the Coast Guard Squadron III to be used in military action along the coast of South Vietnam against enemy positions. At the end of this turbulent existence, the *Duane* was finally pensioned off into her well-deserved retirement. Now she rests on the ocean bottom; the memory of her heroic feats lives on among the divers who visit her.

## THE DIVE

Although the sea is quite rough during our visit, the big yellow marker buoy over the wreck can still be seen from a long way off. Our instructor holds the briefing while we are still in relatively calm waters on the Florida Bank. After attaching *Ocean Diver II* to the mooring buoy, we complete our preparation for the dive. A taut cable connected to the platform helps the group reach the buoy, where they enter the deep waters. Like almost all the wrecks in

B

C

the Caribbean, this site has enormous barracuda circling the buoy line. The outline of the *Duane* appears slowly out of the dark blue that surrounds us. We reach the quarter-deck and our reaction is one of wonder: the ship is truly enormous. I realize immediately that an in-depth exploration will require several dives. Although the wreck has been on the sea bottom for only a few years, there is already a lot of vegetation covering it. The first superstructures we see are adorned with big gorgonians, whose dark red colors are lighted by our torch beams. We can make out a high structure, the eagle's nest, around which a group of jacks and several barracuda are swimming. Their silhouettes against the light are magnificent. Moving along the parapet of the wreck, sheltered from the current, we come to the chimney stack and head for the equipment at the center of the ship. The view from the flying bridge, above the upper deck, is spectacular. The bulwarks plunge vertically downward on both sides; they, too, are completely clothed in soft corals, among which huge parrotfish search intently for food. A shoal of blue-black surgeonfish pays diligent attention to the action in front of the bridge. Just beneath me, where some steel panels have given way, two enormous eyes are staring up; they belong to a brown grouper over 3 feet (1 meter) long. I would gladly stay here for hours, but my dive computer tells me the time has come to head for the surface.

Looking around, it's clear that anything that could damage the environment or harm scuba divers has been removed—all the metal cables and struts, along with all the doors. On the way back to the surface, we take another look at the bridge. We are just reaching the ship's interior

D

*A. The wreck of the Duane is visible in the clear water; this photo was taken just after it sank. You will need more than a single dive to explore this huge wreck.*

*B. The huge propeller lies at a depth of 108 feet (33 meters). Specific preparation is required to reach it.*

*C. The bridge superstructures are entirely covered in dense incrustations of colorful organisms.*

*D. Most of the metal structures are perfectly preserved.*

*E. Smallmouth grunts (Haemulon chrysargyreum) swim undisturbed on the inside of the bridge, which has become a huge aquarium.*

E

from the bridge through what was once a door. There is nothing left of the ship's instrumentation, but the animals and vegetation are more interesting anyway. An enormous shoal of snappers grudgingly leaves us room to get through, preceding us inside. A diffused light shines through the portholes, and the flashlight beams pick out the magnificent colors of the bulkheads and ceiling. The foredeck is just as intriguing, but will have to wait for another dive. A trip to the propeller is exciting, too, but requires special preparation because of its depth.

The wealth of vegetation shows that the currents around the *Duane* are considerable, and you will need more than just basic training to dive here. The most important thing to do is enter and exit close to the buoy. You can also explore the wreck from the sheltered leeward side.

# Key Largo: Dry Rock—
## The Christ of the Abyss

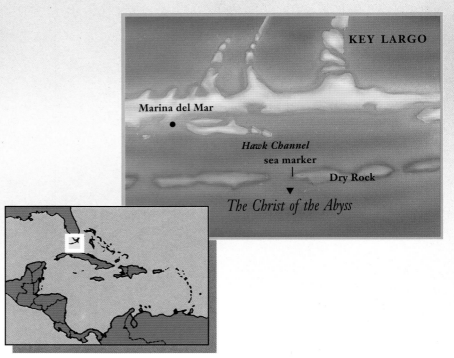

KEY LARGO

Marina del Mar

*Hawk Channel*
sea marker

Dry Rock

▼

*The Christ of the Abyss*

0 m
0 ft

4.5 m
14 ft

7.5 m / 25 ft

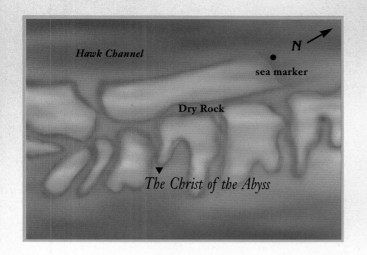

Hawk Channel

sea marker

N

Dry Rock

*The Christ of the Abyss*

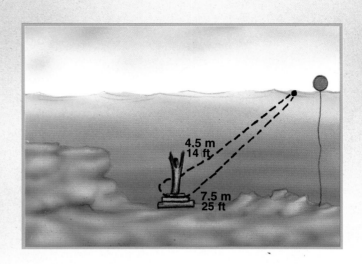

4.5 m
14 ft

7.5 m
25 ft

Dry Rock, one of the best-known dive sites in Key Largo's marine park, is home to the sanctuary's symbol, the statue of the Christ of the Abyss. It is not in the open sea, like Elbow or Molasses, but lies northeast of Marina del Mar, a popular dive site with 12 permanent buoys. This is an ideal place for snorkeling because the coral reef almost reaches the surface of the water.

of barracuda live here permanently, including Smoky, who is 5 feet (1.5 meters) long and loves the camera. The last time I was here I didn't see him, but all the dive masters were sure that it was only a temporary absence and that he would eventually find his way back to Dry Rock.

A

B

C

D

*A. This picture will look familiar to divers who have seen the statue of Christ of the Abyss in Italy, which has been protecting divers at San Fruttuoso, off Genoa, since 1954.*

*B. The incrustations and the clarity of the water are very different, but the effect of the image is the same in Florida as in Italy.*

*C. Big barracuda are a permanent presence on the Dry Rock sea bottom. They are happy to approach divers and allow them to take close-up photographs.*

*D. Divers at Dry Rock will find themselves surrounded by compact crowds of yellowtail snappers (Ocyurus chrysurus).*

The statue rests on a cement base at a depth of 25 feet (7.5 meters), with the coral barrier extending to the right and left of it, forming a kind of canyon. The place teems with fish, untroubled by the numerous divers. Apart from the usual coral fish, you will sometimes meet big shoals of yellowtail snappers swimming in formation above the reef among the elkhorn coral and around the statue.

The corals around the statue form a maze of canyons and tight corridors, which are worth a close look. They are the natural habitat not only of invertebrates but of big prawns and lobsters. Large numbers

F. *A large adult male stoplight parrotfish* (Sparisoma viride) *proudly shows its lively colors.*

G. *An indigo hamlet* (Hypoplectrus indigo) *swims in front of a forest of sea plumes.*

H. *At the bottom of the reef, a Florida stone crab* (Menippe mercenaria) *threateningly charges out from the door of its den.*

E. *Snappers, grunts, and goatfish often form mixed shoals that take shelter among the massive corals.*

## THE DIVE

Key Largo's Christ of the Abyss figure, with upstretched arms, is a copy of a statue I have seen in the Mediterranean. Located on the sea bottom at San Fruttuoso, near Genoa, Italy, the original is the work of Guido Galletti; it was lowered to the sea bottom in 1954 to represent the patron saint of divers, fishermen, and all sea-going people. This bronze copy, like the original, is almost 10 feet (3 meters) tall and weighs 3,965 pounds (1,800 kilograms). It was cast from the same mold to be presented to the American Underwater Society by Egidio Cressi, the Italian dive-equipment manufacturer.

Here, yellowtail snappers and bright blue parrotfish search the base of the statue for food. Depending on the position of the sun, the statue provides a series of different backdrops for great pictures. Today, during our morning dive, the sun is still far to the east and the figure of Christ is a powerful image against the light. After taking some photographs, we head into the canyon to explore the surrounding rocks, which form a vertical wall. Dry Rock has no strong currents and, although this makes diving easier, visibility is a few meters less than on the outside of the reef. The most striking sights are the many large brain corals and the numerous shoals of snappers.

# Key Largo:
# Molasses Reef

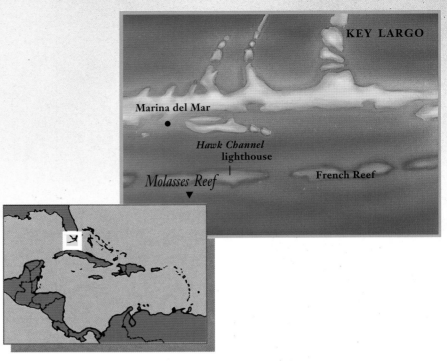

KEY LARGO

Marina del Mar

*Hawk Channel*
lighthouse

*Molasses Reef*

French Reef

0 m
0 ft

3 m
9 ft

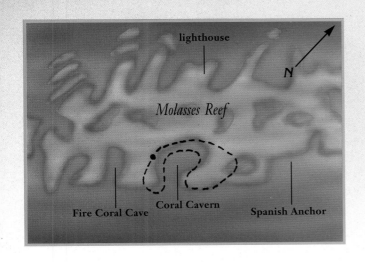

lighthouse

*Molasses Reef*

N

Fire Coral Cave     Coral Cavern     Spanish Anchor

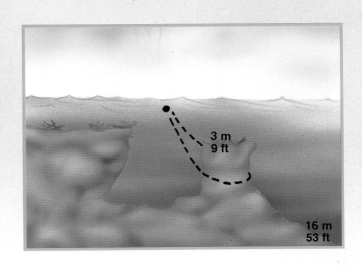

3 m
9 ft

16 m
53 ft

## LOCATION

Molasses Reef is a favorite among divers visiting Key Largo. This stretch of the coral reef, at the southern perimeter of the marine sanctuary, is spectacular. The wreck of the *Duane* is nearby, and alongside it there are many other ships wrecked against the dangerous coral barrier reef. Today, Molasses Reef has a big lighthouse. The Gulf Stream brings clean, fresh water, making visibility wonderful and attracting large pelagic fish from the open sea. Although there are no drop-offs to great depths here, the barrier is rich in canyons and sandy clearings. The plateau starts close to the surface of the water and then goes straight down to a maximum

*A. Spanish Anchor, evidence of how dangerous Molasses Reef once was for ships. Today the reef is marked by a lighthouse.*

*B. Wide gorgonian fans grow tall to take advantage of plankton-rich currents.*

depth of about 56 feet (17 meters). The Miniwall plunges vertically at some points and masses of fish congregate beneath it. There are numerous hollows and tunnels to explore; in fact, Molasses Reef is impressive all the way from Fire Coral Cave to Miniwall to the Wellwood side, no matter where you start your dive. Spanish Anchor, a huge anchor on the sea bottom close to Hole in the Wall, makes an interesting photograph when shot with a diver in the background for scale.

*C. A small group of Atlantic spadefish* (Chaetodipterus faber) *reflects the bright rays of the sun.*

*D. A whitespotted filefish* (Cantherines macrocerus).

## THE DIVE

The powerful boats of the dive operators get you the 6 miles (10 kilometers) to Molasses Reef in no time. You generally get about an hour underwater, after which the boats move to another anchor site to change the tanks, giving you another hour underwater. And they still have you back in time for lunch!

The late summer day of my dive is hot and perfectly still as Molasses Reef appears before us in all its beauty. Visibility is perfect and the water is so flooded with light that I have to adjust the aperture and set the fastest exposure time possible to get a dark enough background for my shots. I swim slowly along the reef. There are brown elkhorn corals growing as far as the eye can see along the edge of the wall and on the plateau; they look like giant fingers. These corals are common in both the Caribbean and in the Western Atlantic; the shallow reefs of the Florida Keys from Key Largo to Key West are their natural habitat. They are very fragile and divers must move along the reef carefully, paying attention to how they move their fins. There are always small groups of fish shaded in the corals: French grunts, bluestriped grunts, and white grunts. I even manage to find a trumpetfish, hiding stiff and unmoving between the coral branches, waiting for prey. Two big French angelfish have been following me for a few minutes, but whenever I try to get in close for a shot, they disappear into the coral. They return immediately, but keep out of the way of the camera, teasing me. All the members of this family are here, from the gray angelfish to the gaudy queen angelfish. It is like being in an aquarium: wherever you look there are fish of all colors and kinds, from moray eels to

groupers. There is plenty of movement out in the open sea, too. Along with the yellowtails, at least 8 Atlantic spadefish (*Chaeteodipterus faber*) swim above the corals. They look like, but have no relation to, the batfish of tropical seas, and can grow up to 1.5 feet (.5 meter) long. You will find that time and film run out much too quickly at Molasses Reef.

E. *A shoal of colorful yellow grunts, made up of several species, swims close to the reef. Notable are* Haemulon chrysargyreum *and* Haemulon flavolineatum.

F. *A trumpetfish* (Aulostomus maculatus) *camouflaged among the branches of a gorgonian.*

G. *A French angelfish* (Pomacanthus paru).

H. *A queen angelfish* (Holacanthus ciliaris) *swims close to a huge barrel sponge.*

I. *A few schoolmasters* (Lutjanus apodus) *swim in their usual habitat among gorgonians and elkhorn coral.*

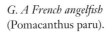

# CUBA

While United States federal law prohibits travel to Cuba, many divers are understandably tempted to visit. Each year, thousands arrive, giving in to the lure of Cuba's magnificent bays, beaches that stretch 4,350 miles (7,000 kilometers), and some of the best

Havana

CUBA

Trinidad

CARIBBEAN SEA

Camagüey

CABEZERIA DE
CAYO BLANCO

ISLA DE LA
JUVENTUD

CAYO LARGO

LOS JARDINES
DE LA REINA

Santiago de Cuba

diving in the entire Caribbean. The island perches on the edge of the Mexican trench, so its ocean floor is richer in life than almost any other. Like most Caribbean sea beds, the shallow waters are dominated by gorgonians and the deeper waters by sponges. This domination of species is testament to the Caribbean Sea's independent evolutionary course, its isolation from other oceans for millions of years. There are sponges of all shapes and sizes, from minute, invisible ones that bore tunnels into coral so they can live inside it, to the huge

A

B

C

A. The island of Cuba is surrounded by thousands of smaller islands with coral sands and turquoise seas, still essentially unexplored.

B. Gorgonians of differing shapes and species can be found, depending on environmental conditions.

C. Gorgonians dominate wide tracts of the sea bed with their branches.

*D. Most of the organisms in this picture are gorgonians.*

*E. The bright colors of the sponges are a central attraction of the Caribbean.*

*F. A school of blue tang (Acanthurus coeruleus) moves over the reef looking for seaweed.*

"elephant's ears" that grow up to 10 feet (3 meters) in diameter.

There are plenty of good dives off the Cuban shoreline, but the most interesting sites are along the edge of the continental shelf, which often runs close to the coast. The renowned Isla de la Juventud has been a magnet for divers for decades; Cayo Largo and Los Jardines de la Reina are 2 sites recently discovered by divers. Conditions

G

H

D

E

F

are great almost all year round in these waters, except September and October. From May to November, the weather is hot; the rest of the year is more temperate, with lowest temperatures of about 75°F (24°C) in January and February.

In the centuries after 1492, when Europeans believe Columbus discovered Cuba, the island became so famous for piracy that it was here, on the Isla de Pinos (now Isla de la Juventud), Robert Louis Stevenson used as the setting for Treasure Island. Among the real pirates was Pie de Palo (Pegleg), who was paid by the French and English governments to undermine the Spanish hegemony in South America. He amassed fabulous treasures by attacking the loaded ships returning to Spain. Some say he hid his treasure here, perhaps underwater.

*G. The fairy basslet (Gramma loreto) is one of the best known and most colorful species of fish in the Caribbean.*

*H. The gray angelfish (Pomacanthus arcuatus) is the largest angelfish in the Caribbean, measuring up to 20 inches (50 centimeters) long.*

# Isla de la Juventud, Cuba:
## Cabo Francés

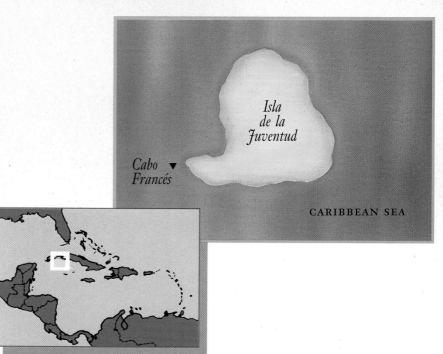

Isla de la Juventud

Cabo ▼
Francés

CARIBBEAN SEA

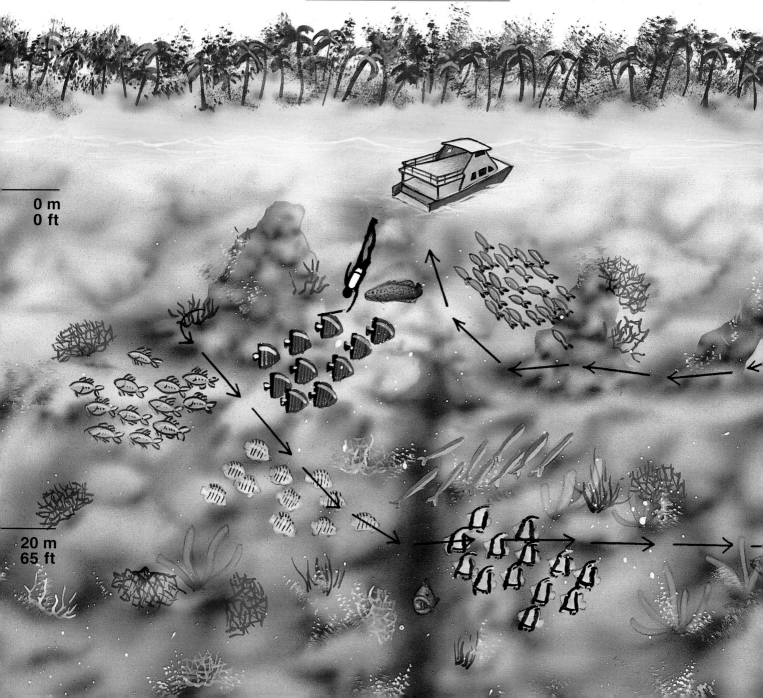

**0 m**
**0 ft**

**20 m**
**65 ft**

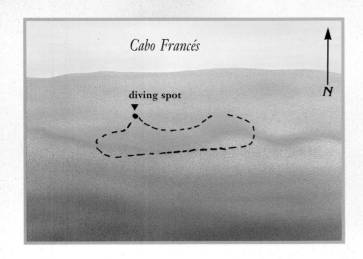

Cabo Francés

diving spot

N

20 m
65 ft

## LOCATION

The dive sites at Cabo Francés are a 45-minute trip from the marina on one of the fast support boats owned by island's only dive operator. There is a night dive every week and two dives a day: the first along the outer reef wall, the second on the platform behind the reef. Divers stop for lunch and a rest between dives at The Rancheron, a restaurant on a platform above the stunning white beach. Look into the water from the platform to see shoals of yellow snappers around the support piles.

A

B

*A. A shoal of French grunts* (Haemulon flavolineatum) *surrounds a squirrelfish.*

*B. The gray angelfish* (Pomacanthus arcuatus), *although common, never ceases to fascinate divers.*

*C. A school of schoolmasters* (Lutjanus apodus) *swims slowly above the rich coral beds that surround the Isla de la Juventud.*

*D. Some schools of big tarpon* (Megalops atlanticus) *are non-migratory and can be found consistently in the same place on a reef.*

*E. Big tube sponges* (Agelas sp.) *are common to all dives in the Caribbean.*

C

D

E

## THE DIVE

Cabo Francés offers some of the best diving in Cuba. For years, Isla de la Juventud has lured divers from all over the world with its transparent water, great depth, and giant sponges. In fact, the underwater photography world championships were held along the stunning wall of this island. You can dive along this same wall for weeks and see something new each time. It plunges right off the continental shelf and, after about 1,000 feet (300 meters), drops more than 3,280 feet (1,000 meters). A series of buoys stretches along the edge to mark the dive sites. Buoys #1 to #34 indicate dives along the wall, and the others indicate shallower dives on the reef behind the wall. The edge starts at 65 feet (20 meters) and disappears thousands of feet (several hundred meters) into the deep blue. The sponges vary endlessly in shape but not in size; they are all giant and rule the wall. Look at them closely and you will see that they are not just huge and inert things, but growing animals, reproducing and fighting amongst themselves. Close to buoy #4 in particular, you will find several sponges engaged in a silent but deadly battle for space and light.

There are caves along the wall, some of them very large and reaching to a depth of 165 feet (50 meters); the cave near buoy #7 is especially interesting. Through the top of the cleft you can see the Caribbean tarpon with their huge silver scales, swimming slowly against the illuminated backdrop of the water's surface. You can swim down the "tunnel of love," a deep vertical cleft lined with gigantic sponges.

Behind the wall is the coral plateau, which is no deeper than 50 feet

with their curly tentacles and for transparent and purple prawns. Groupers come here often to have their mouths painstakingly cleaned by the prawns; you will see them floating about patiently with their mouths open.

At buoy #56, whole forests of beautiful purple gorgonians live on the walls of a gully that descends from 35 feet (10 meters) to 50 feet (15 meters) to the sandy floor. An unusual number of splendid flamingo tongues, mollusks found only in the Caribbean, live here on the branches of the coelenterates.

G

F

H

(15 meters); many hard corals grow on its sandy bed. Lots of tarpon gather around a huge coral arch at buoy #38, and squads of fish swim unceasingly under a rocky arch about 13 feet (4 meters) high. Groupers are everywhere and easy to approach, especially at buoy #40, where they are often brought food by divers. You may see surgeonfish here, too. El Cabezo Solitario (buoy #46) is a lone reef populated by plenty of crustaceans that live by cleaning parasites from other animals. Look into the nooks and crannies for the sea anemones

*F. The yellowline arrow crab (Steno-rhynchus seticornis) is easily identified by its disproportionately long legs.*

*G. In the areas of the reef exposed to constant weak currents, it is not uncommon to see the branchial crowns of feather duster worms (Bispira brunnea), which quickly withdraw at the slightest vibration.*

*H. A huge gorgonian lifts its wide fan toward the surface.*

# Cayo Largo, Cuba:
## Cabezeria de Cayo Blanco

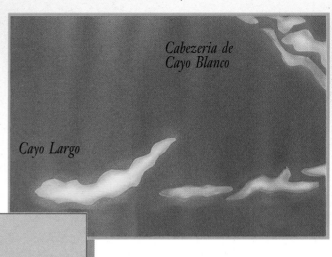

Cabezeria de
Cayo Blanco

Cayo Largo

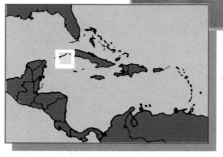

0 m
0 ft

10 m
30 ft

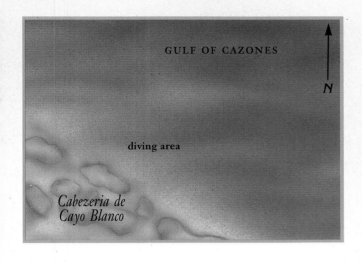

GULF OF CAZONES

N

diving area

*Cabezeria de
Cayo Blanco*

10 m
30 ft

## LOCATION

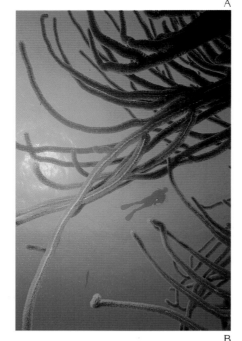

Cayo Largo is in the Los Canarreos archipelago, which is the only surface-breaking part of the huge, low-lying Jardines de la Reina Bank (the last strip of Cuban territory before the Gulf of Mexico). The dive potential of this island is clear from studying its marine charts. The southern coast reaches a depth of 3,280 feet (1,000 meters) just over .5 mile (1 kilometer) from the shore, and a deep channel runs north of the archipelago between the Jardines Bank and Cuba. Its

walls drop vertically to 656 feet (200 meters) and run for miles before disappearing into the Gulf of Cazones. The Cabezeria de Cayo Blanco, a long stretch of reefs and sand spits that disappear at high tide, lies along this wall. Where the sea bed plunges, there is a wealth of marine life, including big predators in the early months of the year. The best period for diving in the Gulf of Cazones is from June to December, when the prevailing wind is east-southeast.

*A. The branches of sea-rod gorgonians, covered with thousands of polyps that filter the nutrient-rich water for nourishment.*

*B. A southern stingray* (Dasyatis americana) *swims over one of the wide sandy clearings that link the numerous reefs of the Cabezeria.*

*C. A gigantic tube sponge* (Aplysina fistularis) *provides contrast to the sea plume behind it.*

*D. Two sponges rising from the same base look like signposts.*

*E. A large vase sponge can conceal fish and other organisms.*

## THE DIVE

It is difficult to pinpoint one specific dive site along the Cabezeria; the whole wall buzzes with life and is relatively new to divers. Most of the Cabezeria is suitable only to experienced divers because the current is often very swift and strong; many dives use the drift system. Beginners should stay in the shallower levels, where they will still be able to see the big oceangoing predators. This is big predator country: sharks (including the whale shark), eagle rays, and jacks will almost reach the sur-

face here. Most divers feel they are exploring an unknown sea bed. You will find corals, sponges, and gorgonians, and be surrounded by masses of fish including giant dentex, tropical groupers, and nurse sharks. The sheer quantity and size of the fish—giant groupers, sea bream so big that they live with remoras, eagle rays, and stingrays—will tell you that this sea has rarely been touched by humans. Cayo Largo has just been discovered by divers in the last few years, and only a tiny fraction of the Los Canarreos sea bed has ever seen a diver.

*F, G. Sponges seem determined to reach their maximum size in the Caribbean, forming substrates on which small gorgonians can establish.*

*H. A school of Atlantic spadefish* (Chaetodipterus faber). *Note the distinctive dark bands, which differ from one individual to another.*

*I. A pair of spotted eagle rays* (Aetobatus narinari).

# Los Jardines de la Reina, Cuba: Octopus Lair

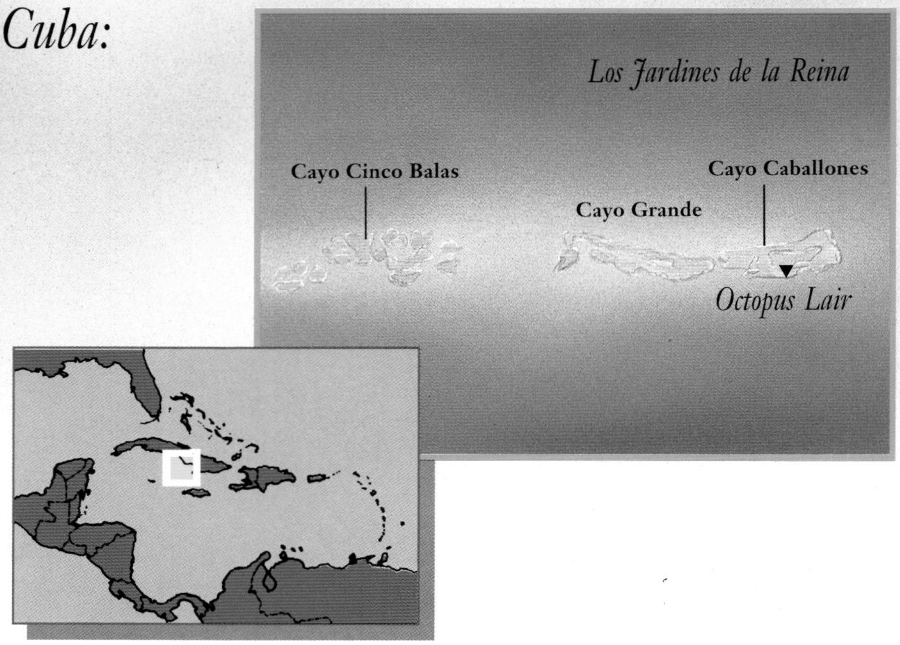

Los Jardines de la Reina

Cayo Cinco Balas

Cayo Grande

Cayo Caballones

Octopus Lair

0 ft

50 ft

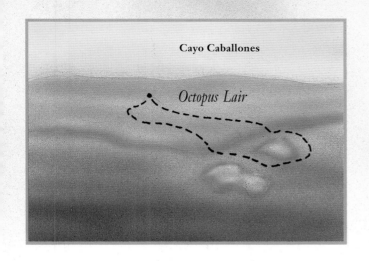

**Cayo Caballones**

*Octopus Lair*

15 m
50 ft

A

A. *These peculiar gorgonians, called sea plumes, can grow to heights of over 6.5 feet (2 meters) in several different habitats.*

B. *Numerous plankton-feeding organisms, such as gorgonians and sponges, grow along the steepest parts of the reef wall. Here is a beautiful pink vase sponge (Callyspongia plicifera).*

C. *Big barracuda (Sphyraena sp.) often swim close to the reef, drawn by the wealth of marine life.*

D. *The silvery tarpon (Megalops atlanticus) can be unusually big—over 6.5 feet (2 meters) long.*

## LOCATION

Los Jardines de la Reina archipelago comprises more than 200 cays stretching in an arc over 125 miles (200 kilometers) parallel to the south coast of Cuba. Its coral reef is among the longest in the world, and many years of isolation have made it one of the most unspoiled dive sites in the Caribbean. Separated from the mainland by the Golfo del Ana Maria, it is just a few hours by boat from Marina de Jucaro, not far from the small town of Ciego de Avila. The archipelago is uninhabited; the only way to explore the reefs is with a dive cruise.

C

D

B

## THE DIVE

One of the best dives in the archipelago is Octopus Lair. It is a huge crater 50 feet (15 meters) deep and about 40 feet (12 meters) in diameter, with neat piles of rocks along the edges, like the lair of a giant octopus. There is no giant octopus, of course, but you will see a spectacular green moray *(Gymnothorax funebris)* and lots of small reef fish, especially grunts *(Haemulon sp.)*, gregories *(Stegastes sp.)*, and chromis. The crater is usually the first stop on the dive schedule; then you move on to the banks of coral and gorgonians in the surrounding area and admire the huge resident shoals of grunts *(Haemulon flavolineatum, Haemulon sciurus,* and *Anisotremus virginicus)*, the butterflyfish, and the ever-present trumpetfish. Farther down, there is a landslide of reefs covered with corals,

*E. The green moray is nocturnal. During the day, it will often allow divers to approach it in its den.*

*F. Tiger groupers* (Mycteroperca tigris) *often hover immobile in the water. Although shy, they are quite curious about divers and will let them approach.*

*G. One of the amazing underwater panoramas at Octopus Lair. As in other parts of the Jardines de la Reina, underwater life is plentiful, thanks to its relative isolation.*

*H. All the reef walls are encrusted with marine organisms.*

including the huge black bush species and many sponges of the genera *Aplysina, Callyspongia,* and *Xestospongia.* The sponges are home to a fascinating selection of animals: morays *(Gymnothorax moringa* and *Gymnothorax miliaris)*, emperor fish *(Holacanthus ciliaris)*, French angelfish *(Pomacanthus paru)*, sea anemones *(Bartholomea* and *Condylactis)* with their resident cleaner prawns, giant crabs *(Mithrax spinosissimus)*, and lots of other interesting species. This is a good dive to repeat after sundown, when you will often see the elegant flamingo tongues *(Cyphoma gibbosum)* and the surreal arrow crabs *(Stenorhynchus seticornis)* on the gorgonian sea fans.

# MEXICO
## *Cozumel*

A

B

The Mexican island of Cozumel, 8 miles (12 kilometers) off the northeast coast of the Yucatan peninsula, is small, just 29 miles (46 kilometers) long and 9 miles (14 kilometers) wide. It is the largest of the 3 islands (Cozumel, Mujeres, and Contoy) that front the northeastern coast of Mexico. The underwater world of Cozumel is part of Belize Reef, the world's second-largest reef, which stretches 200 miles (320 kilometers) from the southern tip of Mujeres to the Gulf of Honduras.

The pre-Colombian history of Cozumel evolved parallel to the rise and fall of Mayan civilization. Spaniard Don Juan Grijalva discovered the island while trying to reach Cuba. In the years that followed, the Spaniards used the island as a base for their attacks on the Mexican mainland. Some fearsome pirates operated out of Cozumel during the sixteenth century, including the infamous Jean Lafitte and Henry Morgan. Two hundred years of piracy devastated the small groups of peaceful Mayans and Spaniards, who abandoned the island in 1843. In 1848, fishermen and farmers from the troubled mainland fled to Cozumel and started its repopulation. Chewing gum (of all things), invented in the United States around 1900, turned the island into an industrial center.

During World War II, the Americans built an airstrip and a submarine base on the island, where Marine Corps divers trained for upcoming events in Europe and the Pacific. It was these men who returned to Cozumel after the war for pleasure and who spread the word about the extraordinary diving there.

## DIVING ON COZUMEL

The entire Cozumel coast is open for tourists, but practically all the dive sites are on the west, leeward coast. The reef surrounds the entire island, but it is impossible to dive the east coast because of the massive breakers. The waters off the west coast are generally calm, except when the north-northwest winds blow in late fall. You can dive from

*A. A series of intersecting passages meander through massive coral towers into the reef.*

*B. Incredibly architectural coral structures and brightly colored sponges are the main characteristics of the reef's shallower surfaces.*

the beach; at points where the reef narrows, the drop-off is a 165-foot (50-meter) swim away.

The island boasts at least 20 dive shops where you can rent equipment (with a diver certification) and get a list of all the shore access points. Until 10 years ago, all dives were made from small boats and it used to take a day to do 2 dives on the southern and northern reefs. Today, faster dive boats allow you to do a 2-tank boat trip before lunch, along with afternoon and night dives.

The Guyana current, flowing north, strikes the southern tip of Cozumel, producing secondary currents of varying intensity. The constant currents generally flow south-north, but they can change direction suddenly. Most boat dives use the drift technique and are supervised by expert local dive masters. CADO (Cozumel Association of Dive Operators) regulates all dives, with the following requirements:

- 40 bar (500 psi) minimum tank air pressure
- 130-foot (40-meter) depth limit
- No decompression dives
- 3-minute safety stop at 16 feet (5 meters)
- No removal of anything

Underwater, Cozumel is similar to the northeastern Caribbean. The reef has 3 basic sections: shallow reef, medium reef, and drop-off reef. The entire area, especially close to the medium and drop-off reefs, is broken up by canyons at right angles to the coast (called sand shuts), which were excavated by masses of melted water during the Ice Age. Today, corals and sponges create a fantastic seascape. Thanks to the currents, the waters are always transparent and visibility is often over 165 feet (50 meters). Water temperature is constant at around 77°F (25°C) in winter and over 85°F (29°C) in summer.

There is a rich variety of fish: eagle rays, barracuda, jacks, and graytip and blacktip sharks are common around the medium reefs and drop-offs. Schools of stingrays rest on the sandy floor, and enormous nurse sharks hide in the nooks and crannies all along the reefs. You will notice that it is the angelfish who are the real masters of the reef, hovering in every corner. There are snappers, too, especially on the intermediate reef. You may encounter the splendid toadfish *(Sanopus splendidus)*, a species found only here; it hides in the reef during the day and swims the top of the reef at night. Don't touch them—they have a swift and terrible bite. You will hear the snapping of their jaws frequently during night dives.

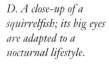

*C. A very unusual encounter in these waters: a splendid toadfish* (Sanopus splendidus), *with the characteristic striped head, peculiar shape, and long barbels underneath its mouth. This fish is dangerous and may bite when touched.*

*D. A close-up of a squirrelfish; its big eyes are adapted to a nocturnal lifestyle.*

*E. Big, solitary barracuda* (Sphyraena sp.) *hunt the sea bed of the reef.*

# Cozumel: Santa Rosa Wall

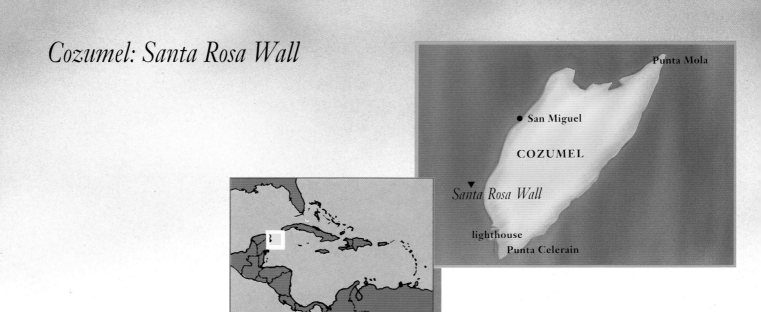

Punta Mola

San Miguel

COZUMEL

*Santa Rosa Wall*

lighthouse

Punta Celerain

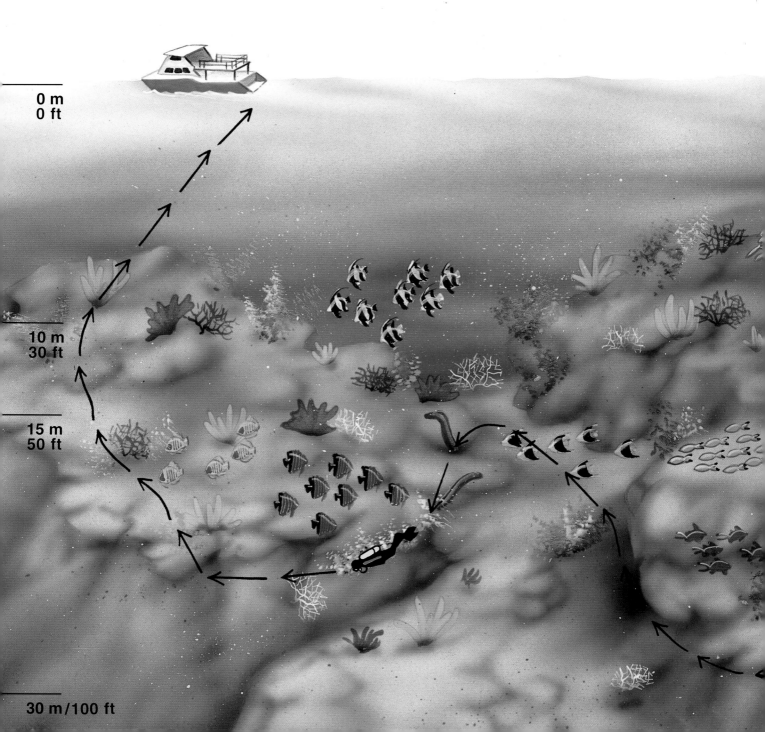

0 m
0 ft

10 m
30 ft

15 m
50 ft

30 m/100 ft

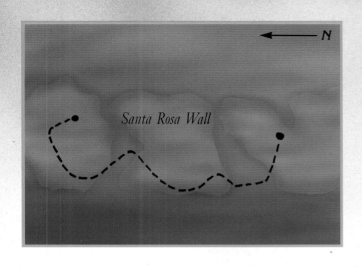

Santa Rosa Wall

N

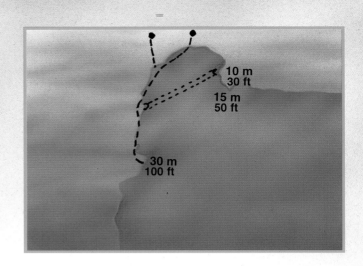

10 m
30 ft

15 m
50 ft

30 m
100 ft

A

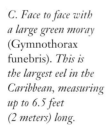

B

C

D

## LOCATION

This is the most northerly of the 3 Cozumel dive sites described here. It is such a long reef that, even with favorable currents, it is impossible to swim on one tank. The current normally flows south-north, but it is very strong and unpredictable. You can find shelter from it in one of the many passages that lead straight to the reef. The down currents can be a nuisance; they flow toward the coral platform and push you down the sheer wall

*A. Big yellow tube sponges* (Aplysina fistularis) *grow well along the steep walls.*

*B. The sponges, an element of every dive, always make the brightest blotches of color.*

*C. Face to face with a large green moray* (Gymnothorax funebris). *This is the largest eel in the Caribbean, measuring up to 6.5 feet (2 meters) long.*

*D. This enormous sponge is an elephant ear. Unmistakable, this variety grows all over the steep Santa Rosa Wall.*

of the reef to the ocean bottom. Do not inflate your stabilizer jacket in these conditions. Keep calm and use your fins to push yourself hard to the reef, where the current will pass you by, allowing you to slip into one of the many canyons.

The south part of the reef slopes only slightly, but in the north the Santa Rosa Wall plummets from the reef platform—about 30 to 40 feet (10 to 12 meters) deep—to breathtaking depths. If you get the right tunnel, you can swim through the reef and look straight down into the abyss at the exit. The wall is covered with deepwater gorgonians, whip corals, and sponges. There are enormous orange elephant-ear sponges and yellow tubes over 3 feet (1 meter) long. Fantastic tunicates can be found among the black coral formations or on the branches of dead gorgonians. At depths of over 65 feet (20 meters), it is the landscape that is most interesting; in shallower waters, it is the fish. You can see green morays (*Gymnothorax funebris*) stretching out of their dens and enormous black sea groupers (*Mycteroperca bonaci*). Sometimes there are whole schools of spiny lobsters underneath the canyon rims.

## THE DIVE

As is usual here, our boat drops us behind the reef. We head west over the slightly sloping pale sand, and the first dark shadows of reef appear in the distance. Sand shuts through the wall lead straight out onto the slope.

The bottom of the canyon is covered in snow-white sand, and the walls of the reef above are decked with soft corals and sponges. The brilliant colors of the rope sponges are in stunning contrast to the blue

*E. The branches of this deepwater gorgonian are entwined with the branches of a red rope sponge.*

*F. A yellowline crab* (Stenorhynchus seticornis) *is easily recognized by its long legs; it is lying on an orange sponge.*

*G. The splendid toadfish* (Sapodus splendidus) *is one of the main attractions at Cozumel. This species has never been seen anywhere else.*

of the water. Still inside the passage, we cannot feel the current yet, but the air bubbles from another group of divers demonstrate the speed of the water in front of the sheer outer wall. The current soon catches us as well, carrying us along slowly and inexorably. It is a tremendous experience to abandon yourself to the current and allow it to carry you along the reef wall. From a distance, I spot two enormous sponges under an outcrop on the reef; they make a good photograph against the deep blue water.

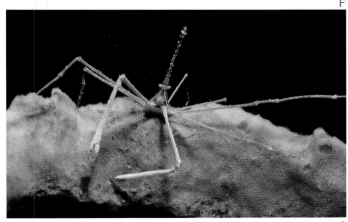

With a few fin strokes I am close to the reef where the current is very weak, no longer a problem for photographers. The water is so clear that we can see well below the depth we have fixed for the dive. The temptation to let yourself go down into the blue expanse is great, but don't succumb.

Three huge black groupers lead us through a canyon to the reef. It must be their territory; they are making circles around us. They use every passage and tunnel in the reef and seem to be everywhere, all the time, and not just in front of the lens. Our 45 minutes are up and this is where our boat will pick us up, so we stop for our compulsory 5 minutes at 16 feet (5 meters).

*H. Large black groupers* (Mycteroperca bonaci) *are quite common below 65 feet (20 meters), where they hang immobile in the water, well clear of the bottom.*

*I. The first part of the reef ends in a sandy platform. Divers can take time to admire the shapes and colors of the organisms on the encrusted wall.*

# Cozumel:
# Palancar Caves

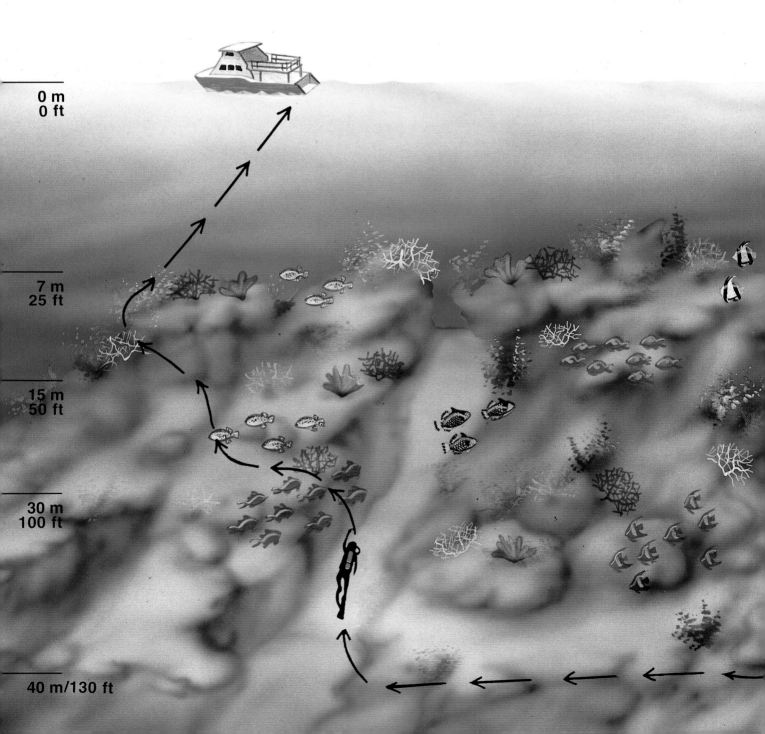

Punta Mola

● San Miguel

COZUMEL

▼ Palancar Caves

lighthouse

Punta Celerain

0 m
0 ft

7 m
25 ft

15 m
50 ft

30 m
100 ft

40 m/130 ft

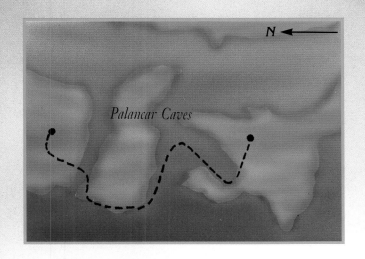

Palancar Caves

N

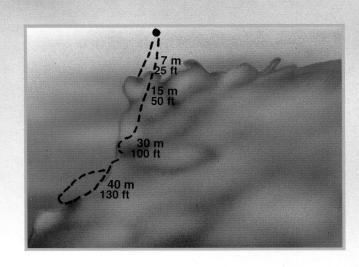

7 m
25 ft

15 m
50 ft

30 m
100 ft

40 m
130 ft

## LOCATION

The Palancar Cave system stretches nearly 3 miles (5 kilometers) and is one of the favorite dive sites on Palancar Reef at Cozumel. In this area, the reef does not plunge straight down to the sea bed at every point; there are long flat sections, known as the Palancar Shallows. Farther north is another section of the reef, the Palancar Horseshoe. The Palancar Caves are separated from the shallows by a sandy trench that varies in depth from 23 to 33 feet (7 to 10 meters).

drops sheer to a depth of about 98 feet (30 meters) on a sandy slope that leads to the drop-off. The real drop is farther than the permitted depth, which in most dive sites is between 98 and 130 feet (30 and 40 meters). In this part of the reef the current is light to medium; visibility is generally between 98 and 165 feet (30 and 50'meters). There are some particularly unusual types of fish to see here, including filefish, boxfish, red-finned parrotfish, pufferfish, and spotted drums.

*A. The Palancar Caves are a maze of hollows, tunnels, and canyons inside coral towers.*

*B. The amazing tunneled landscape of the Palancar Reef provides plenty of opportunities for underwater photographers to combine natural and artificial light.*

*C. A large stovepipe sponge (Aplysina archeri).*

*D. A large black grouper (Mycteroperca bonaci).*

The wide structure of the Palancar Caves is as full of holes as Swiss cheese. Canyons and sand shuts are crisscrossed by a labyrinth of holes, tunnels, and coral towers. The roofs of the tunnels are covered mainly with brilliant orange sponges. There are significantly fewer soft corals here than anywhere else on Cozumel, probably because of the damage caused by hurricane Gilbert in 1988. The landscape is extraordinary and the freedom of swimming in and out of the blocks of reef is exhilarating. The outer reef wall

## THE DIVE

After the drop, the water is crystal clear. Visibility is over 165 feet (50 meters)—perfect conditions for diving in the Palancar Caves. It is the underwater scenery that takes your breath away here; the caves are not particularly rich in fish.

The south-north current is virtually imperceptible. To get an idea of the bizarre reef formation, we purposely swim a few meters above the reef platform. Innumerable canyons and troughs tempt us and it is hard to decide where to start. We slide along the bottom of a canyon hidden by a huge outcrop. Underneath it, there are weird sponges, and farther back we see a crack that shelters 3 large, spiny lobsters. Because of the incredible visibility, we choose to get an overall impression of the area rather than focus on details. The wall drops away at the canyon exit, where the walls of the reef, decorated with enormous gorgonians, rise upward. The gorgonians look almost black to the eye and reveal their true red only when lighted by strobe or torch. We are at the foot of the reef now, at a depth of 98 feet (30 meters). This is where the very steep sandy bottom starts, stretching to the drop-off. Running out of time, we see a tunnel ending in a point that we would like to explore. The sun's rays filter in through a narrow slit in its roof, reflecting an enchanting blue light on the sand. (Drift diving is a great advantage for divers who like to spend a long time taking photographs and admiring the seascape.) We travel with the current and reach the surface at the set time. The exit from this pretty blue grotto leads into the sandy expanse behind the reef, where we have plenty of time to look for stingrays and other fish.

*E. A shoal of bluestriped grunts* (Haemulon sciurus) *swims slowly along the sea floor.*

*F. A spotted trunkfish* (Lactophrys bicaudalis) *examines the photographer.*

*G. A young female parrotfish showing the lively colors that mark her age and sexual development.*

*H. The Caribbean spiny lobster* (Palunirus argus) *finds an ideal environment in Cozumel waters.*

# Cozumel:
# Columbia Wall

Punta Mola

● San Miguel

**COZUMEL**

*Columbia Wall*
▼
lighthouse

**Punta Celerain**

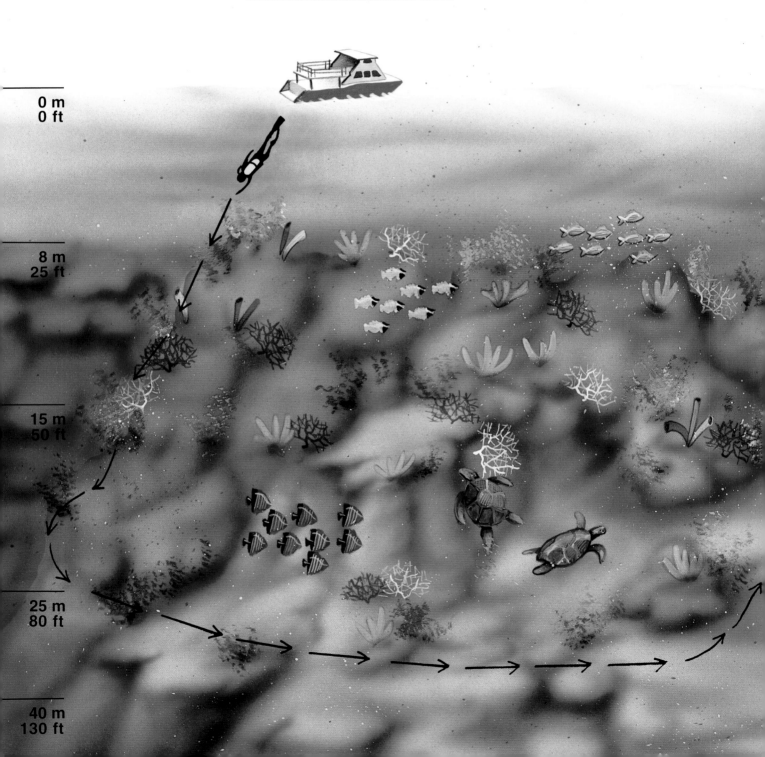

0 m
0 ft

8 m
25 ft

15 m
50 ft

25 m
80 ft

40 m
130 ft

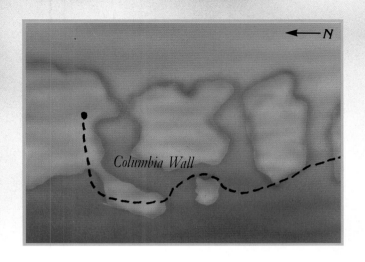

N

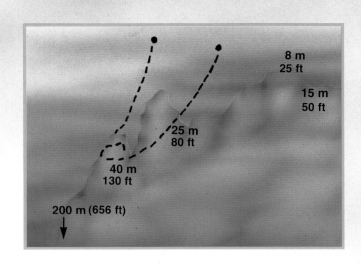

8 m
25 ft

15 m
50 ft

25 m
80 ft

40 m
130 ft

200 m (656 ft)

Columbia Wall

## LOCATION

Columbia Wall is between Punta Sur Reef and the southern tip of the Palancar Reef. This area has a really spectacular drop-off, with massive coral towers that grow to the surface from depths of up to 60 feet (18 meters). The reef is very wide here, starting from a depth of between 20 and 26 feet (6 and 8 meters) and continuing in a single, unbroken slope to the sheer wall. Canyons and pathways run the width and length of the coral block, leading right to the edge of the drop-off

*A. A series of arches looks like a natural path through the Columbia Wall reef.*

*B, C. Divers take time to admire life on the reef while being carried along by a medium current.*

*D. The biggest caverns in the Columbia Wall maze are dominated by dense schools of silversides. Their silvery bodies reflect the filtering light.*

ledge—one of the reasons a maximum depth of 98 feet (30 meters) has been set for dives along the wall.

This dive site does not have just an amazing underwater landscape; there are plenty of fish too. You will see huge formations of yellowtail snappers, Bermuda chub, and jacks. It is not unusual to see turtles, groupers, and eagle rays either. During certain periods, blacktip sharks appear on Columbia Reef and stay for several weeks.

The surfaces of the reef, canyons, and outcrops are all covered with rich vegetation. Gorgonians cling to the sheer outer wall. Any kind of sponge will grow here; the most striking are the various and colorful tube sponges. The luxuriant vegetation and great quantity of fish are the result of the almost ever-present current, which varies in intensity from medium to strong. Because of this current, the dive is suitable for expert divers only. The water is generally very clear, but strong currents will occasionally bring a lot of particles. Suspended particles don't affect visibility, but do appear as white spots on a photograph taken too close or with too bright a strobe.

## THE DIVE

Today we want to explore as much of Columbia Wall as we can. We have a wonderful dive master, Enrice, who knows the reef intimately, and we know the dive is going to be exciting. We have planned our hour-long dive carefully with our dive computers to give us the best possible ratio between depth and time. We enter the water close to the shallowest part of the reef and reach the first coral blocks after a few meters. In some places, the coral formations go more than a meter under the surface; we will be able to spend a long time here on ascent. We move quickly toward the drop-off. Enrice points out an outcrop farther down on the reef where there is an entire shoal of silver-gray snappers. They stare wide-eyed into the camera, unmoved by the flash. At this point the reef slopes gradually down and the depth is already 50 feet (15 meters). We have some idea of the topography from Enrice's sketch and know that the drop-off is not far away. We swim to the edge of the ledge and experience the fantastic sensation of

E

*E. A spotted eagle ray (Aetobatus narinari), with its unmistakable shape and coloring, emerges from one of the reef tunnels.*

F

G

H

drop-off diving. We let ourselves sink down to 98 feet (30 meters) and swim slowly along the wall, supported by a fairly strong current. In front of us there are gorgonians and soft corals growing straight out into the sea. We look up. The reef wall, with its strange outcrops, seems like a huge curtain through which we can look into the open sea.

Our bottom time passes all too quickly and we begin to ascend slowly toward the tunnels and hollows of the coral masses. Enrice leads us in a twisting path across one canyon taking us inward, and then to another that takes us out. He also knows a series of crossways that takes us through the reef in an erratic path; they are all wide enough to cross without touching the sides or the bottom. We arrive, euphoric, back at the boat. Columbia Wall has shown us its best.

*F. A forest of gorgonians waves slowly in the current at the edge of the drop-off.*

*G. A large turtle swims slowly, propelled by wide, paddle-like fins.*

*H. A shoal of horse-eye jacks (Caranx latus) patrols the reef. They sometimes approach divers spontaneously, attracted by the air bubbles and the glitter of the apparatus.*

# THE CAYMAN ISLANDS
## *Grand Cayman*

**G**rand Cayman, between Cuba and Central America, is a beautiful, almost inordinately tranquil island. Little Cayman, which Columbus called Las Tortuga because of its huge turtle population, made the Caymans a favorite with Spanish sailors, who stocked up on fresh turtle meat here (drastically deplet-

CAYMAN ISLANDS

GRAND CAYMAN

Georgetown

LITTLE CAYMAN

CAYMAN BRAC

*A. Tall sea plumes (Pseudopterogorgia sp.) spread themselves in the current. They belong to the same family as the gorgonians, although they don't look alike.*

*B. A group of bluestriped grunts (Haemulon sciurus) is easily recognized by the blue stripes and black tails.*

A

B

ing the turtle population). Later maritime maps called the islands *Las Cayman*, from a local word meaning "little crocodile." Sir Francis Drake described the islands as uninhabited by humans and populated by huge serpents called *caymanas*.

During a struggle between colonial powers in the Caribbean, the English legalized piracy, hiring privateers to attack Spanish ships. When peace was declared in the Caribbean in 1713, piracy was ended. The last of the pirates, including Blackbeard, took refuge on Grand Cayman, and even today there are rumors of hidden treasure.

An incident known as "the wreck of the 10 sailing ships" occurred in 1788, greatly influencing Grand Cayman's future. Strong winds drove the flagship of an English merchant fleet onto the eastern tip of the reef, and all 10 ships sank. Heroic islanders managed to save all the passengers and crew, and in gratitude the British awarded its colony "freedom from tax in perpetuity." Within a few years, the Caymans became one of the major offshore financial centers, attracting countless investors. This financial growth has played a decisive

role in the development of tourism. Today Grand Cayman has hotels, boardinghouses, apartments, condominiums, its own airline—and, incidentally, the best infrastructure for scuba diving in the world.

### DIVING IN THE CAYMANS

There are suitable dive sites around the entire circumference of Grand Cayman. West Bay, where the reef fronts the coastline along Seven Mile Beach, has the greatest concentration of hotels and is the most popular dive site. This side of the island has the calmest waters, and diving goes on all year round. There are some splendid dive sites along the north coast (North Wall West off North Sound). However, they are a long way from the mainland and the success of a dive depends on weather conditions. East End has spectacular seascapes, but is not yet very well developed for diving. These dive sites, too, are a long way from shore, and you will need a powerful boat to reach them. South Shore, 22 miles (35 kilometers) long, is on the west side of the island, within reach of all

**CUBA**

Santiago de Cuba

C. A diver closely observes a splendid composition of large tube sponges.

D. Stingrays can raise clouds of sand with their powerful wing beats.

boats for all-day excursions, which include 3 long, deep dives. There are live-aboard dive boats all around the island.

Grand Cayman's reef lies very close to the coast, except for the huge North Sound lagoon. For the most part, the coast consists of flat rocks that disappear into the water (though Seven Mile Beach is sandy). The ocean floor on Cayman is typically Caribbean: shallow reef, medium reef, and deep reef. On the drop-off, known as "the wall" here, the reef descends vertically for several thousand meters. Perpendicular to the reef there are deep gullies and hollows filled with corals; these make excellent dive sites, especially on the wall.

Grand Cayman is home to the entire range of Caribbean fish. Some species are so numerous at certain sites that the locations are considered "marine miracles" (for example, Stingray City and Tarpon Alley). The water is beautiful, with visibility of 165 feet (50 meters) guaranteed. Temperature is practically constant: 80°F (27°C) in summer and 75°F (24°C) in winter. Many of the dive sites are free from currents, but even where currents do occur they are not a problem for divers.

dive boats. You can dive off the rocky coastline from George Town to Queen's Monument along the South Sound. Sunset House is an extraordinary place to visit, and a dive center there provides rental air tanks. The reef is unique—a treat for underwater photographers. You may encounter a tourist submarine during a dive. Grand Cayman has 111 dive sites, most equipped with permanent moorings.

Rules in the Cayman Marine Park are extremely strict. It is absolutely forbidden to fish, shoot, or pick up anything from the ocean floor. Where there are no mooring buoys, the anchor must be dropped on the sand. Dive masters ensure

that the environment is respected during all dives. Dives are regulated by the Cayman Islands Watersports Operators Association and their rules apply to dive technique (not much different from international norms), standards for dive masters and skippers, and safety equipment. All dive centers hire certified dive masters and skippers exclusively, and all dive boats carry oxygen, VHF radio, and first-aid equipment.

A day of diving in the Caymans starts with a 2-tank trip lasting 3 to 4 hours—a deep dive and an ascent in shallow water. In the afternoon, boats go out for a single-tank dive. Night dives are always available. Many of the dive centers have large

# Stingray City

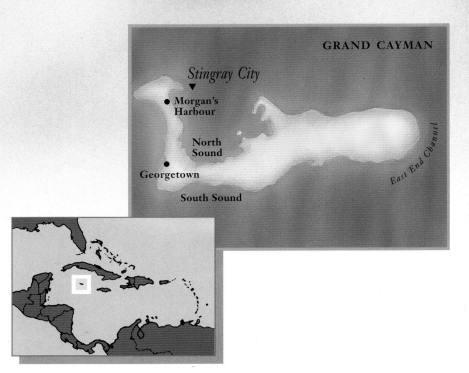

GRAND CAYMAN

Stingray City

● Morgan's Harbour

North Sound

● Georgetown

South Sound

East End Channel

0 m
0 ft

5 m
15 ft

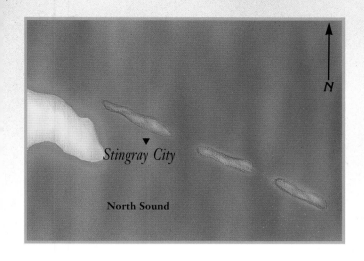

*Stingray City*

**North Sound**

N

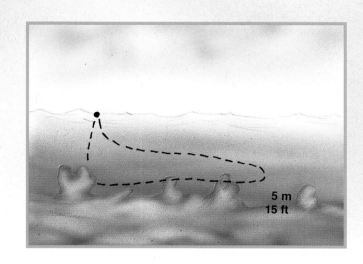

5 m
15 ft

## LOCATION

Stingray City is one of the most famous of all dive sites. Located in the lagoon behind the reef, not far from the entrance to the North Sound, its enormous sandy expanse lies 16 feet (5 meters) deep, protected from the wind and waves. Fishermen were the first to notice and rejoice in the concentration of stingrays here. Curious scuba divers responded to their accounts in 1987 and could hardly believe their eyes. Vast numbers of rays *(Dasyatis americana)* surrounded them, showing no fear or aggression.

Numbers increased as the divers fed the rays, and soon safety and training procedures were introduced. Gloves and knives are strictly forbidden. The animals are given only sardines and octopus brought by the dive masters. The technique for sharing the food properly is clearly explained to visitors, since feeding a ray is more difficult than you might think. Designed to eat off the sea floor, the rays' mouths are on the underside of their bodies; they cannot see the food offered by the divers, but can only smell it. Dive masters demonstrate how to use a closed fist to guide the animal's nose toward the food, releasing it at the right moment. Many of the adult stingrays have become pushy and like to knock divers onto the sand, but they are completely harmless. They never use the sting on their tails; in all these years, not one of the thousands of visitors has been hurt. Marine biologists can see no negative consequences of the practices at Stingray City. In fact, numbers continue to increase, especially of males and babies. No one has been able to make an accurate count, but hundreds of stingrays thrive here.

A. *One of the many dive boats that ferry divers to Stingray City.*

B. *Southern stingrays* (Dasyatis americana) *are visible from the surface.*

C. *The stingrays show no fear at all, swimming gently around divers and looking for food.*

D. *The sea floor at Stingray City is home not just to the stingrays, but also to bar jacks* (Caranx ruber), *black surgeonfish* (Acanthurus sp.), *and yellowtail snappers* (Ocyurus chrysurus).

## THE DIVE

To avoid long journeys, many dive centers keep a boat moored at North Sound specially for the Stingray City dive. Our trip across the flat lagoon takes only 30 minutes. Stingray City is behind the reef in the breakers, and to the east there is only one channel that links the North Sound to the open sea. Here in the lagoon, the water is perfectly calm and transparent. The sea bed is flat and the dark stains visible on the bottom are individual blocks of coral scattered all over the white sand.

As soon as we put our feet into the water, a whole group of rays closes in on us just like an aircraft squadron. They are all sizes and colors, from the dark adults to the light-colored babies. In a short time, they have surrounded us like big birds. It does not take them long to identify Kevin, our dive master, who is carrying the food. He demonstrates the feeding procedure and we can see how experienced he is. Kevin practically takes the biggest of the rays by the nose and pushes the food into its mouth. Then he distributes the food to us. I swim around the edges of the action to take photographs. Stingrays are still coming in from all directions, mainly in groups of three or more. I have no food, so they quickly lose interest and move off.

The coral blocks on the sand are inhabited by groupers and big moray eels, who also get some of the food handed out by the divers and live here permanently. We are not the only visitors. There are groups of divers kneeling all over the sand, sharing out food to apparently famished stingrays. Despite the hordes of visitors, diving at Stingray City is tranquil and well organized. It is a dive suitable for beginners and even snorkelers.

*E. Divers can swim in very shallow water with animals their own size.*

*F. Several hundred stingrays can be found together on the bottom of this lagoon.*

# Grand Cayman:
## Babylon

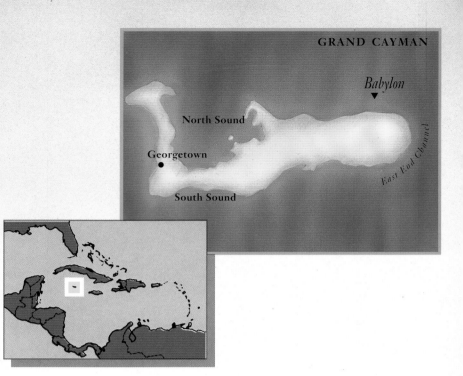

GRAND CAYMAN

Babylon

North Sound

Georgetown

South Sound

East End Channel

0 m
0 ft

18 m
60 ft

30
100

40
130

656

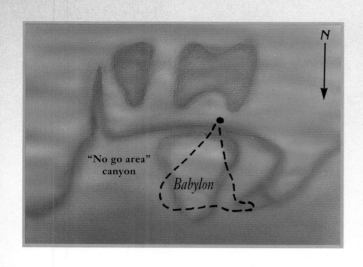

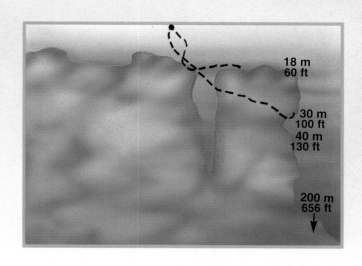

## LOCATION

Babylon is on the west side of the North Wall, a long way from West Bay and South Sound, where most of the dive centers are. Not much diving goes on here, but an increasing number of large dive boats moored at North Sound bring visitors, and live-aboard boats, which can get almost anywhere, are becoming more common.

Babylon is a colossal platform colonized by corals, in front of a sheer wall. Only a narrow canyon

A. A narrow canyon separates the huge coral platform called Babylon from the reef.

B. A photograph captures the 3-dimensionality of this large, almost fluorescent vase sponge as it stands out against the blue.

C. The blocks of rock rising from the sand are transformed into extraordinary colored gardens.

D. A school of snappers (Lutjanus apodus) forms a high wall.

separates it from the reef, which is totally covered in soft corals; to allow their proliferation, it has been declared off limits to divers. The panorama is amazing; these natural wonders should indeed be left untouched. The coral shelf, like the tip of Babylon, is 50 feet (15 meters) deep. From there, the walls drop sheer for thousands of meters. The huge coral base is only part of the spectacular topography. To the west, there is a platform that grows in the water like a huge table. Depending on the dive plan, you may actually swim underneath this table. To the east, there is another huge canyon that leads inside the coral shelf. Traveling through this canyon at the end of the dive allows you to swim right back to the mooring in the sandy area.

The coral vegetation both on Babylon and on the drop-off is fantastic. Enormous corals slant downward in almost symmetrical ranks, making the structure look like a mushroom. From 65 feet (20 meters), there are huge bushes of black corals and gorgonians, some bigger than 6.5 feet (2 meters). On the west side, at around 60 feet (18 meters), there are masses of sea anemones. On the same plateau, there are all kinds of fish and other marine life: angelfish, snappers, parrotfish, and whole lines of lobsters underneath the ledges. In the blue water along the drop-off, schools of black jacks (Caranx lugubris) advance from the depths in perfect formation, and eagle rays propel themselves forward with elegant wing beats along the sheer wall. Underwater photographers need to take 2 cameras with them, a wide-angle lens to capture the extraordinary panorama and a lens with greater focal depth to pick up the tiniest details.

## THE DIVE

We drop anchor in one of the sandy expanses about 130 feet (40 meters) behind the edge of the reef, and plan to swim north to the drop-off. We move off midway between the sea bed and the surface. Horizontal visibility is about 98 feet (30 meters); we can already see the edge of the reef and the pear-shaped top of Babylon outlined against the intense blue of the water. We cross the canyon that separates the edge of the reef from the coral bank. The plateau is to our left at a depth of 130 feet (40 meters). Our dive plan includes a rapid visit to this huge protuberance, a thorough investigation of Babylon, and then a return trip through the canyon. The view is astounding: covered with enormous bladed corals, the rocks look like a man-made monument. This is my first dive on this part of the island and I have the impression that the vegetation is healthier here than in other parts of the island. Pelagic fish, especially jacks, swim by us continually, and a whitetip reef shark swims along the edge of the reef. Sharks are not habitual visitors here on Grand Cayman, which makes this a particularly interesting encounter. Unfortunately, the predator is too far off to capture fully on film, but I am consoled by a gigantic turtle, who heads impassively straight for me. The canyon we take on the return journey is ideal for photographs against the light. Swim below your group of divers to get a good shot with the edges of the gully on the left and right. We make the decompression stop underneath the boat by the deco bar, a ballasted pole at a depth of 16 feet (5 meters). The pole has 2 automatic respirators with pipes attached, supplying enough air for divers whose reserve is running low.

E. A hawksbill turtle (Eretmochelys imbricata) *close to the deep Babylon plateau.*

F. A big snapper with unusual yellow coloring looks at the photographer from its secure refuge in the reef.

G. A formation of horse-eye jacks (Caranx latus), *identified by their yellow caudal fins.*

H. An adult male stoplight parrotfish (Sparisoma viridis), *one of the most common parrotfish, swims among the corals and the sea fans at a depth of about 65 feet (20 meters).*

# Grand Cayman:
## Orange Canyon

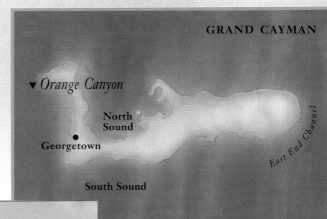

GRAND CAYMAN

▼ Orange Canyon

North
Sound

Georgetown

South Sound

East End Channel

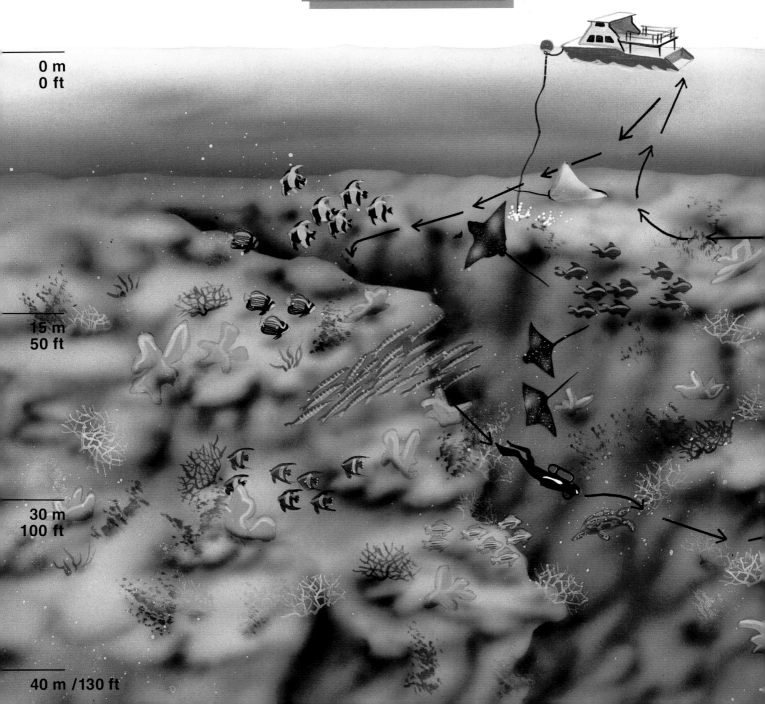

0 m
0 ft

15 m
50 ft

30 m
100 ft

40 m / 130 ft

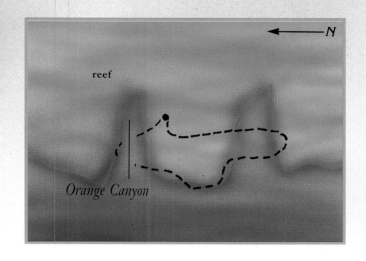

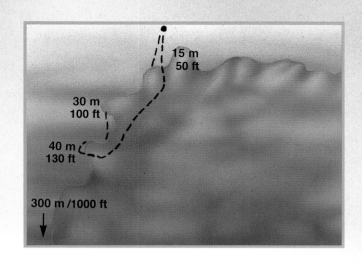

## LOCATION

Orange Canyon is on the west-coast drop-off of the island. The reef looks like a series of massive balconies and terraces overhanging the chasm, which plunges vertically down for thousands of meters. The current varies from light to medium. Big gorgonians flourish here, but the outstanding feature of this dive site is the mass of orange sponges. They grow to impressive sizes and are scattered all over the reef. This is a paradise for photographers who favor wide-angle shots.

Sometimes you will see a group of triggerfish here. They swim using only their back and ventral fins and like to follow divers at a safe distance. On the reef plateau, at a depth of 50 feet (15 meters), visitors can always see a shoal of snappers *(Lutjanus apodus)* and angelfish

moving in pairs. These creatures have completely overcome their fear of people, and will follow you around like puppies. Actually, this can be a nuisance for photographers; they are always trying to get in the picture.

At the drop-off you can see barracuda, turtles, eagle rays, and schools of jacks. Like all the other dive sites on the west coast, Orange Canyon has a permanent mooring buoy to prevent anchors damaging the reef; even though this is an extremely popular site, the reef is intact. Conscientious divers also contribute to its preservation.

A. The empty sand clearings in the midst of the coral emphasize the wealth of life on the rocks.

B. Orange sponges are the dominant motif in Orange Canyon's underwater scenery. In the middle of the picture, a diver observes a gray angelfish.

C. This wide gorgonian sea fan seems to be protecting the big tube sponges.

D. A group of haemulids seems immobilized just above the sea bottom.

## THE DIVE

There is often a current at Orange Canyon, but it is rarely very strong and divers usually have no problem returning to their buoy. Furthermore, you will see more fish and the water will be clearer on days when the current is flowing. Today is one of those days, and visibility is exceptionally good. The reef surface—at a depth of 50 feet (15 meters)—and the jagged line of the drop-off stand out clearly against the intense blue of the water.

We find a pair of yellow-and-black French angelfish waiting for us and they make a beautiful photograph. I see a group of silver snappers grazing on the reef surface. The afternoon sun is in a perfect position and its light is shining not only directly onto the drop-off but also into both canyons. This is where most of the gigantic orange sponges grow; they are best photographed at a 45° angle to the surface. (This also provides enormous depth when a diver is swimming in the background.) I try out several different perspectives and quickly find a well-placed group of sponges. I can even get the boat in the top half of the frame and my partner moves over the reef as we agreed before the dive. Despite the antics of 2 angelfish, who keep swimming in front of the lens, I manage to get the pictures I want without losing too much time.

The exit from the canyon leads straight onto the sheer wall of the reef. The landscape is truly theatrical, like an enchanted forest. Colorful soft corals totally cover the jutting rocks. It is hard to resist the temptation to go deeper. We took a lot of time with the photographs so we dare not go farther than our limit of 82 feet

E

F

G

*E. A shoal of horse-eye jacks (Caranx latus) in search of calmer and richer hunting waters.*

*F. The beautiful and photogenic French angelfish (Pomacanthus paru).*

*G. A pair of barracuda (Sphyraena sp.) show their brilliant silvery bodies.*

(25 meters). We consult our dive computers and go back to the no-decompression limit. A second canyon, much less disjointed and with fewer inhabitants, takes us back inside the reef and from there to the platform. Here, at 50 feet (15 meters), our computer translates the reduced oxygen saturation into a decompression stop of 14 minutes—so we have some time to explore the shallower parts of Orange Canyon.

# Grand Cayman: Three Sisters

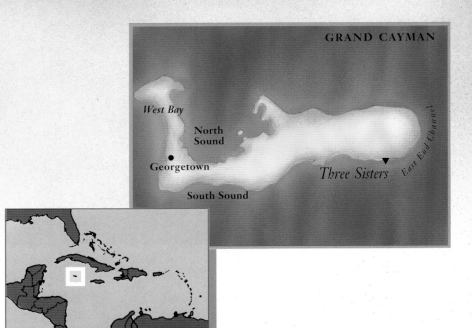

0 m
0 ft

15 m
50 ft

22 m
75 ft

40 m
130 ft

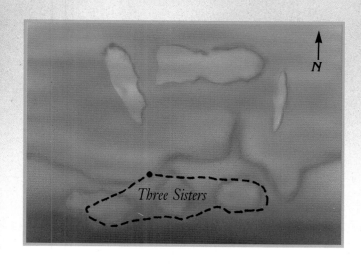

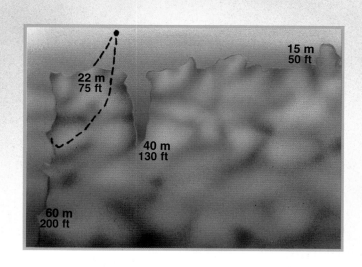

15 m
50 ft

22 m
75 ft

40 m
130 ft

60 m
200 ft

Three Sisters

N

A. The rocky outcrops of the Three Sisters are intersected by deep canyons filled with sponges, gorgonians, and black corals.

B. The deep gorges of the Three Sisters make it possible to go into the canyons from the open sea.

C. A dense colony of sea-rod gorgonians (Plexaurella sp.) stands out against the clear water, through which the outline of the dive boat can be seen.

D. A group of large orange sponges.

## LOCATION

A visit to the Three Sisters requires a long journey. It is almost at the tip of the southwest coast, not far from the corner that leads to the East End Channel. On this part of the island, the drop-offs are deeper than on the West Wall. Here, the reef comes up to only 72 feet (22 meters) below the surface. The Three Sisters consist of enormous rocky plinths in front of the reef wall. You can easily swim through the canyons that traverse them. These canyons are rich in vegetation and care should be taken to avoid damaging the corals.

Plan your dive carefully: the masses of coral are spread out over about 265 feet (80 meters). Your calculations must include the distance from the dive boat to the edge of the reef. To save air and time, you should travel along the drop-off in the open sea, rather than on the reef, at a depth of about 16 feet (5 meters). This will also give you a good view of the sea bed and make orientation easier. You can also go directly through the canyon, which is really spectacular and reaches a considerable depth, but you will use a lot of time and air.

The Three Sisters are rich in vegetation and brilliant with deep-sea gorgonians and sponges. Orange elephant ear sponges are everywhere and huge tube sponges rise in the open sea like cannons. The fish and animals are varied, and near the East End Channel you will probably see large fish, including eagle rays, sharks, and other predators. This is a paradise for divers: a bizarre landscape, rich vegetation, and crystal-clear waters. However, because of the depth and strict dive plan, it is recommended only for experts.

## THE DIVE

The dive master's briefing is very important and deals not only with time and depth, but with the dive route and the configuration of the sea bed. It is also important to the group's safety and confidence. The currents, entrances, exits, emergency procedures, and other subjects are explained in detail. Our briefing was so precise that we have no problem keeping to the dive plan. We intend to get the most out of the Three Sisters.

We drop anchor on one of the sandy expanses about 130 feet (40 meters) behind the reef and start our dive. We can already see the huge rock rising from the depths. It is virtually square and separated from the reef wall by a deep canyon. We descend onto the plateau to a depth of 72 feet (22 meters) and begin to explore.

I immediately see shoals of Creole wrasse *(Clepticus parrae)*. They are purple, which indicates that they are young, and will eventually have a yellow tail. I find a notable specimen of a sea perch under the jutting sheet corals. It is a tiger grouper *(Mycteroperca tigris)* and it observes the camera curiously. Swimming across the coral-filled canyon, we see another group of divers, who have chosen the shorter, deeper route through the canyon to the drop-off.

Now we can see the second of the Three Sisters. It is narrower and ends in a point, like a huge finger. There are a lot of gorgonians framed in fantastic silhouette against the sunlight. Below me, the sea bed drops away into the depths and I abandon myself to the sensation of floating in a void. The journey to the third rock is longer than we thought. It is bigger and just as

E. *Young Creole wrasse* (Clepticus parrae), *identified by their purple color, swim close to the surface of the reef.*

F. *A green turtle* (Chelonia mydas) *rests on the bottom with 2 large remoras.*

G. *Some reef sharks* (Carcharhinus perezi) *stop briefly at a sandy beach near the reef.*

fascinating as the other two. We can only spend a short time exploring the top of the rock because we have stayed a long time at depth.

Two big green turtles *(Chelonia mydas)* rest quietly among a group of soft corals. Although marine turtles have lungs and must return to the surface to breathe, these two look as if they arrived here long before we did. It is not unusual to meet marine turtles on Grand Cayman, even though they were nearly wiped out by the first sailors here and are still

at risk from an operation called the "Cayman Turtle Farm." This company removes turtle eggs from their natural environment, incubates them, raises the young, and then slaughters them for their meat when they are grown. Because marine turtles are now in danger of extinction, many countries have instituted an export ban and the turtle farm has lost much of its international standing. Ecologically minded divers consider it a dubious tourist attraction, and decline to buy turtle steaks and souvenirs there.

# BELIZE

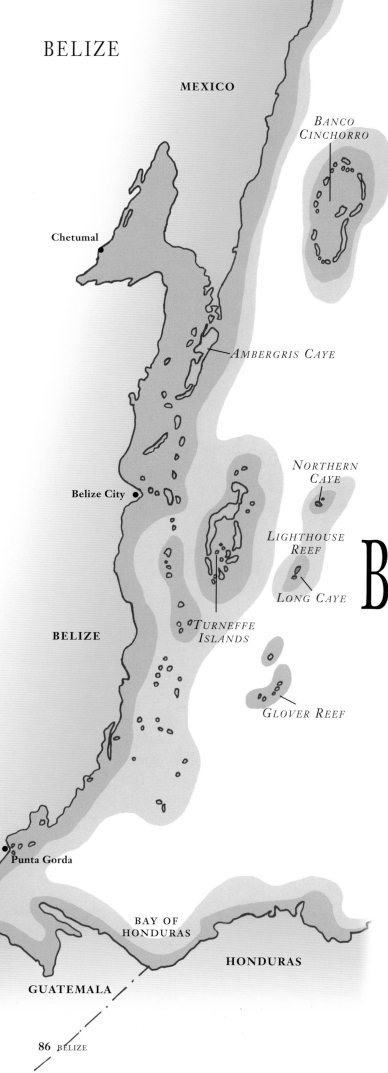

MEXICO

BANCO CINCHORRO

Chetumal

AMBERGRIS CAYE

NORTHERN CAYE

Belize City

LIGHTHOUSE REEF

LONG CAYE

TURNEFFE ISLANDS

BELIZE

GLOVER REEF

Punta Gorda

BAY OF HONDURAS

HONDURAS

GUATEMALA

Belize, formerly British Honduras, is on the Caribbean coast of Central America. It has a surface area of 8,880 square miles (23,000 square kilometers) and a population of 180,000. The northern part of the country is relatively flat, with dense forests and swampy regions. The Maya and Cockscomb mountain ranges, surrounded by miles of grassy meadow, dominate the south.

The Belize reef, second only to the Great Barrier Reef in Australia, stretches for 175 miles (282 kilometers) along the coast. Three isolated reefs lie to the east: those of Lighthouse Reef, Glover Reef, and the Turneffe Islands.

Centuries ago, Belize was an outpost of the Mayan Empire during its classical period. Columbus sailed into the Bay of Honduras in 1502, but its occupation by Europeans didn't begin until 1638, with the arrival of shipwrecked sailors and

*A. In Belize, the calm, sandy waters between the reef and the mainland are scattered with little islands covered in mangroves.*

*B. A solitary coral islet in the throes of formation, just visible as a white stain among the surrounding reefs.*

pirates. Emigrants from the British colony of Jamaica followed. The extraordinary abundance of mahogany and other hardwood trees stimulated interest in the country, and a thriving industry grew up in the eighteenth century. The Baymen, inhabitants of the Mosquito Coast, felt increasingly threatened by the Spaniards who had already colonized land to the north and south. The

C

D

C. *The gray angelfish* (Pomacanthus arcuatus) *is one of the most attractive species in the Caribbean. It is the largest angelfish in these waters, growing up to 20 inches (50 centimeters) in length.*

D. *A diver and an angelfish approach a group of huge sponges.*

Baymen won their last bloody battle on St. George's Cay, and the territory was annexed to Jamaica and called British Honduras. After a government was established in 1961, the country changed its name to Belize. Since 1981, it has been an independent state and member of the Commonwealth.

Belize coasts have fantastic dive sites. A massive reef located 8 to 15 miles (13 to 24 kilometers) off the mainland offers divers a practically untouched underwater paradise. The reef runs parallel to the coast; between them are calm, sandy waters scattered with mangrove-covered islets called "cays." To the east, a deep marine trench separates the 3 coral reefs of Turneffe, Glover Reef, and Lighthouse Reef. It is here that you will find the best dive sites.

The flora and fauna are virtually identical to those of the rest of the Caribbean, although there are some unique differences in type and behavior. For instance, thousands of groupers return every year to the same place to mate, stingrays spend their honeymoon period here, and dolphins visit regularly to observe the humans.

The rich and varied corals and fish reflect the reef's favorable off-shore position in an ocean rich in currents. Divers along the outside edge of the reef are stunned by its plummeting walls, which drop more than 3,280 feet (1,000 meters). Water temperatures are practically constant year round—74° to 77°F (23° to 25°C) in winter and 77° to 83°F (25° to 28°C) in summer—so a $3/16$-inch (5-mm) wet suit is sufficient protection from the cold.

Practically all the beach resorts on the islands along the reef have dive centers, which offer half- or full-day dive excursions. There are also comfortable live-aboard boats, which offer unlimited day and night diving.

# Belize: Blue Hole

Sandbore
Caye

lighthouse

Northern
Caye

White Pelican
Caye

Halfmoon
Caye

lighthouse

Blue Hole

Long
Caye

Hat
Caye

40 m
130 ft

145 m/475 ft

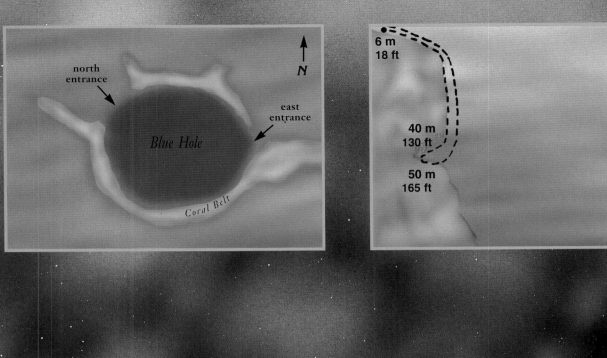

north entrance

Blue Hole

east entrance

Coral Belt

N

6 m
18 ft

40 m
130 ft

50 m
165 ft

145 m
475 ft

A. *An enormous, perfectly circular blotch of dark blue in the middle of the sea indicates a blue hole.*

B. *Below the edge of the Blue Hole, big stalactites stand out against the blue.*

C. *The stalactites hanging from the vault of this ancient cavern feel like milestones on a dive into the past.*

D. *The light seems to disappear in a labyrinth of columns in the Blue Hole.*

## LOCATION

Blue holes are not rare in the Caribbean; you can find them on Andros Island and the Great Bahamas, for example. Stalactites (found in the Blue Hole of Belize) indicate that it was once an above-water cavern called a "karstic hollow." Karstic hollows like this one—irregular limestone regions formed during the Ice Age—were eventually submerged. Water pressure caused the cavern roofs to collapse, creating the sink holes we call "blue holes." The Blue Hole of Belize, the biggest of them all, is in the middle of Lighthouse Reef.

Jacques Cousteau revealed the Blue Hole's secret in 1972, when he maneuvered the Calypso inside and explored it in detail with a miniature bathyscope. It is approximately 1,312 feet (400 meters) in diameter and 475 feet (145 meters) deep, and there are two natural entrances big enough for the passage of very small vessels. The walls are vertical, and at a depth of 130 feet (40 meters) you will find gigantic stalactites, some up to 3 meters long, attached to the underside rim, hanging from the roof like enormous pine cones. The Blue Hole has no extraordinary marine life, but a dive into the ancient cavern is an unusual thrill—most divers say they feel transported into the past.

The dive goes to a depth of 130 feet (40 meters) on a sea floor over 476 feet (145 meters) deep, so there are several very strict technical requirements. A detailed briefing to establish route, time, and maximum depth precedes the dive; a dive master usually accompanies divers.

The light that manages to penetrate through the circular aperture is really minimal. Depending on the time of day and weather conditions, visibility can vary from poor to nil. You must bring a torch, not only to see the stalactites, but to locate your fellow divers. Photographers should use 200 ASA/ISO film to make the most of the poor light. Do not use too powerful a strobe: ascending air bubbles cause particles in suspension to break up at face level and they appear on the photographs as white spots. Video cameras, however, must have artificial light to pick out more than just silhouettes of the stalactites.

E. The big pillar stalactites point to the sea floor, 328 feet (100 meters) below.

F. Light filters and reflects through this underwater cavern just as sound echoes through caves on land.

G, H. The torch throws a ghostly light on rocks in the dark cave.

## THE DIVE

The stalactites on the northwest side of the Blue Hole are our first destination, not far from the north entrance. Our dive will also end on the sandy floor of this slightly sloping channel; it is an ideal place for a quiet decompression stop after a deep dive.

Entry into the water is usually marked by a small buoy, with a cable leading to the slope from which the descent begins. We must be careful to maintain perfect buoyancy because we will be hovering over a sea bottom about 495 feet (150 meters) deep. Compared to the walls of the open reef, these look bare, covered with hard, blue-green algae. Although the sun is shining brilliantly above us, at 98 feet (30 meters) the light is already very poor and we turn on our torches. At 130 feet (forty meters) we can see the black line of the rim, beneath which the stalactites begin. Every diver in the group adjusts his or her buoyancy with extreme precision and we slowly make our way into the darkness. The beams from our torches throw a ghostly light onto the gigantic, cone-shaped forms that hang from the vault. Some are twisted like corkscrews; others are perfectly straight. It is a truly fantastic sight. The background noise coming from the depths is already perceptible and remains a memorable part of the dive. Unfortunately, the time passes too quickly and we slowly swim back to the edge of the reef to begin our ascent. We come out of the Blue Hole at the gently sloping sand channel, a natural passage into the reef. On the surface, under the sun, we appreciate the burst of life all around us; but the Blue Hole made a profound impression on all of us.

# Belize: Long Caye Aquarium

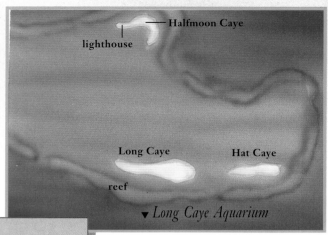

Halfmoon Caye

lighthouse

Long Caye

Hat Caye

reef

▼ *Long Caye Aquarium*

0 m
0 ft

10 m
30 ft

30 m/100 ft

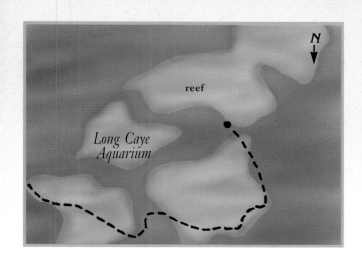

reef

Long Caye
Aquarium

N

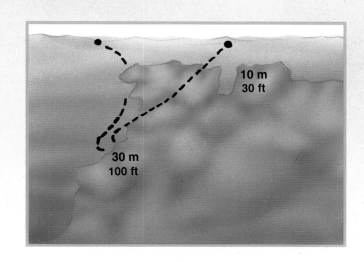

10 m
30 ft

30 m
100 ft

A. *The island of Long Caye is totally covered in dense vegetation, right up to the edge of the beach.*

B. *Great blocks of rock rise from the bottom, decked in sponges, sea fans, and sea plumes.*

C. *Large corals form ideal platforms for these bright red ramified rope sponges (Aplysina sp.).*

D. *The floor alternates sandy tracts with rocks and coral.*

E. *A pair of large gray angelfish (Pomacanthus arcuatus) swims close to the summit of the reef. These fish are not shy and approach divers spontaneously.*

## LOCATION

This is just one of many superb dive sites on the reef west of Long Caye. As its name suggests, the Aquarium offers an astounding variety of fish and brilliantly colored vegetation. The reef surface teems with life at 33 feet (10 meters), so there is no need for a deep dive. The island itself is flat, elongated, and totally covered with low-lying vegetation. Its many salty streams are a great breeding ground for mosquitoes, so bring repellent. There are no resorts on the island, but the base

at Ambergris Caye to the north regularly accommodates groups of tourists for a few days at a time in bungalows and tents. It is an ideal place for divers to stay because the best sites are close to the island.

The water around Long Caye is usually clear and the constant light current ensures plenty of plankton and food; this is why you will see every possible kind of fish here. The sea floor is particularly favorable to divers because the reef surface is not too deep and the drop-off starts at 33 feet (10 meters). However, from this point the wall plunges vertically, broken only by a few small shelves and by outcrops of mushroom coral. Yellow-and-black French angelfish and the beautiful blue-and-yellow queen angelfish are the most common species. Keep an eye on the open sea as you move along the wall: huge shoals of jacks patrol the waters here, along with occasional sharks and eagle rays. The reef has many sand shuts, some actual tunnels and others partially covered with coral.

Photographers will find an interesting subject in the shoals of blue damselfish that graze the coral in loose formation, their amazing blue-violet colors glinting in the light. Green morays live in the canyons, and longspine squirrelfish *(Holocentrus rufus)* hover beneath the reef's outcrops. Shoals of blue-striped grunts *(Haemulon sciurus)* move about over its surface or hover motionlessly in perfect formation below the soft corals.

## THE DIVE

We leave the buoy and swim west to the drop-off. We follow the classic dive pattern, inspecting the widest part first and then ascending slowly, making the most of every minute. The sea floor plummets down before our eyes in a vertical wall covered in soft corals, sponges, and outcrops of mushroom coral. We launch ourselves into the void like expert base jumpers and the sensation is indescribable. We descend the first 98 feet (30 meters) with no difficulty, keeping a strict eye on our time and air reserves. The current pushes us toward the south, so we start the dive from the opposite direction.

Enormous bushes of black coral grow freely in the water. Huge stovepipe sponges, some longer than 6.5 feet (2 meters), wave in the current like the trumpet section of a huge band and often block our way. We look out toward the open sea to see if there are any large fish. Sure enough, an enormous eagle ray slides majestically by before our eyes, propelled by its imperceptible wing motions. We ascend rapidly and discover many more fish at a depth of about 50 feet (15 meters).

The mouth of a chasm that ends in a tunnel opens in the reef wall in front of us. Taking very great care not to stir up the sand or touch the vegetation, we swim through onto a wide stretch of pale sand behind the reef. We are keeping perfect time with our dive plan and head for the reef surface in order to have the full hour's dive.

F

*F. Big, silvery tarpon* (Megalops atlanticus) *are common in sheltered parts of the reef.*

*G. The waters over the drop-off are ruled by big schools of horse-eye jacks* (Caranx latus), *mixed here with yellowstriped rainbow runners* (Elagatis bipinnulatus).

G

*H. A close-up of a large French angelfish* (Pomacanthus paru). *Its yellow eyes are an almost unmistakable feature.*

H

# Belize: Halfmoon Wall—
# The Cheminée

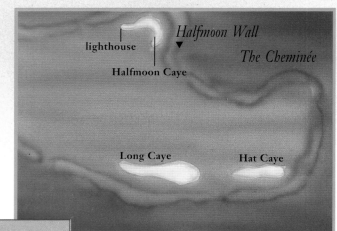

0 m
0 ft

15 m
50 ft

30 m
100 ft

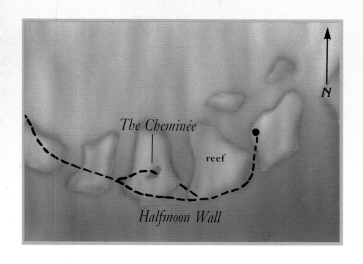

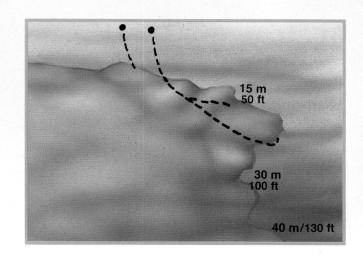

## LOCATION

In addition to some outstanding dive sites, the southeast part of Lighthouse Reef has an idyllic little island, covered with palm trees, with its own lighthouse. This is Halfmoon Caye, named after its shape and now used as a bird reserve. Thousands of red-footed boobies and frigate birds nest in the trees and bushes on the

*A. No other sea can boast the variety of sea fan species and shapes of the Caribbean.*

*B. Halfmoon Island, with its lighthouse near the tip.*

*C. Many forms of benthic life create colorful, intricate landscapes. Divers must keep their distance in order not to damage them.*

*D. The play of the currents has encouraged the establishment of a large number of sea plumes* (Pseudo-pterogorgia sp.) *that have transformed the rock into a gigantic flower.*

southern part of the island; 98 species of birds have been recorded so far. Halfmoon Caye's lighthouse keeper is also the reserve warden. He likes to look out for the tourists and keeps a guest register in which nearly every tourist is entered. He built a platform that rises above the tops of the trees from which you can take excellent pictures of sitting boobies and flying frigates. Bring a telephoto lens with a maximum 200-millimeter focal width.

The start of the dive, known as "the Cheminée" because of its chimney shape, lies off the island's southern coast, next to Halfmoon Wall. A shallow, sandy floor separates the island from its belt of reef, which is relatively narrow at this point. This allows divers the opportunity

to visit the back of the reef, which is in shallower waters, after they have explored the drop-off. Large rays bury themselves in the sand to sleep in back of the reef, and hundreds of garden eels live in the sand; from a distance, they look like a huge asparagus bed, waving in the undertow. When we approach, they shoot back below the sand. The reef surface is at about 50 feet (15 meters), and numerous sand shuts lead straight to the wall. The steeply sloping Halfmoon Wall is truly spectacular and gets the sun practically all day.

The rich vegetation reflects the occasional presence of strong currents in this corner of Lighthouse Reef. Soft corals grow in forests on the surface of the reef, and sponges, black corals, and gorgonians cover the edge of the drop-off, transporting the diver into an enchanted world. The Cheminée has yet another attraction: a natural tunnel in the reef that you can easily cross— if you feel comfortable in narrow, desolate, and dark places.

Divers ascend from a depth of 98 feet (30 meters) to the exit at

E. *Many schools of horse-eye jacks* (Caranx latus) *attest to the richness of the islands' waters.*

F. *A hawksbill turtle* (Eretmochelys imbricata) *swims along the sea floor at Halfmoon Wall. Although this species is common here, encounters are infrequent.*

G. *The most shaded walls are preferred by the ramified sponges, which create lively blotches of color intermingled with the filiform white gorgonians.*

H. *The white, sandy floors are an ideal habitat for southern stingrays* (Dasyatis americana), *which have pointed wings and a long tail armed with large, venomous spikes.*

E

F

G

H

50 feet (15 meters). This is not only technically correct, but provides an opportunity to admire the effect of the rays of light filtering through the surface of the water. There are fish of all varieties here. Keep an eye to the open sea for whitetip sharks and sea turtles, who come to the cay to lay their eggs.

Sponges are a constant presence here. Most common are giant barrel sponges at the rear of the reef, where the vast sandy floor starts. Some are so big you can hide inside, but don't try it—you may damage the sponge.

## THE DIVE

We start from the sandy tract behind the reef belt. From here, we head through one of the numerous canyons to reach the drop-off. In some points, the narrow chasm is right on top of us, totally covered with overhanging soft and hard corals. The water is clear. In front of us we see the exit to the steep wall, against a background of amazingly deep blue. At the very moment that our companions disappear into the darkness, we spot a large shoal of jacks; the filtering sunlight sparkles on their lean bodies. We let ourselves drop, maintaining constant buoyancy, to the planned depth of 130 feet (40 meters) and move along the vertical wall to the east. In some points, the drop-off is so prominent that, looking upward, it creates a curtain against the pale surface. One of our team has fixed two powerful lights to a video camera and their light shows the true marvel of the coral's color. The tubular sponges, which look brown in the twilight of the depths, light into a bright red, and the gorgonians, seemingly an anonymous greenish color, show up as a lively yellow-orange. Unfortunately, our time goes by swiftly and we have to ascend. We pass through one of the numerous canyons in the reef, out onto the sandy expanse to watch the garden eels and the sleeping rays.

# THE HONDURAS BAY ISLANDS
## *Guanaja*

The Bay Islands—Cayos Chochinos, Utila, Roatan, Barbareta, and Guanaja—are 40 miles (65 kilometers) off the north coast of Honduras, the result of a volcanic eruption and the proliferation of corals. Guanaja, where the following dive sites are located, is .5 mile (1 kilometer) wide and 2.5 miles (4 kilometers) long.

A people known as the Payans, closely related to the Mayans, inhabited the islands 600 years ago. Their tranquil existence was interrupted around 1502, when Columbus landed here. He named the islands Islas de Pino, because of their pine forests. They were annexed by the Spanish crown and exploited indiscriminately, their inhabitants massacred. England annexed all the Honduran islands in 1800.

Guanaja is a single rocky mass, with no plains or roads. The only way to travel from one place to another is over the water. The 3 little villages—Bonacca, Savanne Bight, and Mangrove Bight—are either built on stilts or cling to the rock, exploiting every last inch of inhabitable surface. There is a landing strip on the island for small DC3-type planes from Ceiba or Roatan.

Guanaja has plenty of freshwater springs and rivers that provide high-quality drinking water all year round. It is surrounded by reefs that offer dive sites for all levels of ability. The flora and fauna are typically Caribbean—soft corals, gorgonians, feather stars, and sponges. At the drop-off, the sea bed plunges vertically for thousands of yards, and northwest of the island there are underwater lava landscapes to explore. The entire range of Caribbean animal life is present here.

*A. The rugged Guanaja coast.*

*B. A school of bluestriped grunts* (Haemulon sciurus) *swims among a forest of sea plumes* (Pseudopterogorgia sp.), *probably looking for crabs and prawns to eat.*

A

B

BELIZE

BAY ISLANDS

*GUANAJA*

*ROATÁN*

Puerto Castilla

BAY OF HONDURAS

*UTILA*

Trujillo

Puerto Cortés

La Ceiba

GUATEMALA

HONDURAS

# DIVING IN GUANAJA

The Posada del Sol hotel, built in the old Spanish style, has 3 dive boats that ferry divers to the 28 sites. Each site has permanent buoys to prevent damage to the reef, and some of the sea floors are drift-dive sites. The dives are organized on American standards, and the base provides all the necessary services, from a dive shop to film developing. Careful

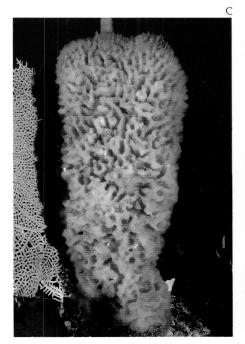

briefing sessions familiarize divers with the site; then they proceed either in independent groups or with a dive master. Respect for the environment is top priority here and the no-gloves rule applies. It is absolutely forbidden to collect mollusks, dead or alive.

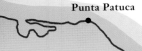

**Punta Patuca**

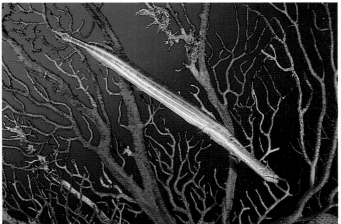

C. These intricate bas-relief sculptures are characteristic of the vase sponge (Cally-spongia plicifera) and its soft tissues.

D. A series of pillar corals (Dendrogyra cylindrus) grow in a tight cluster. Their soft, textured appearance comes from the many polyps that have fully expanded on their surfaces.

E. A streamlined trumpetfish (Aulosto-mus maculatus) camouflaged among the branches of a large gorgonian.

F. A young yellowtail snapper (Ocyurus chrysurus) engaged in a solitary patrol of the reef.

G. Porkfish (Aniso-tremus virginicus) swimming above coral and sea plumes are easily identified by the two black bands on their heads.

# Guanaja:
## *The* Jado Trader

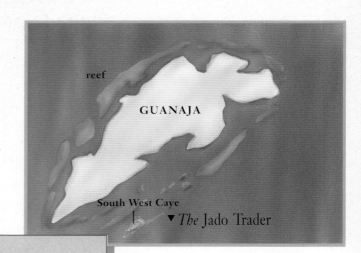

reef

**GUANAJA**

**South West Caye**

▼ *The* Jado Trader

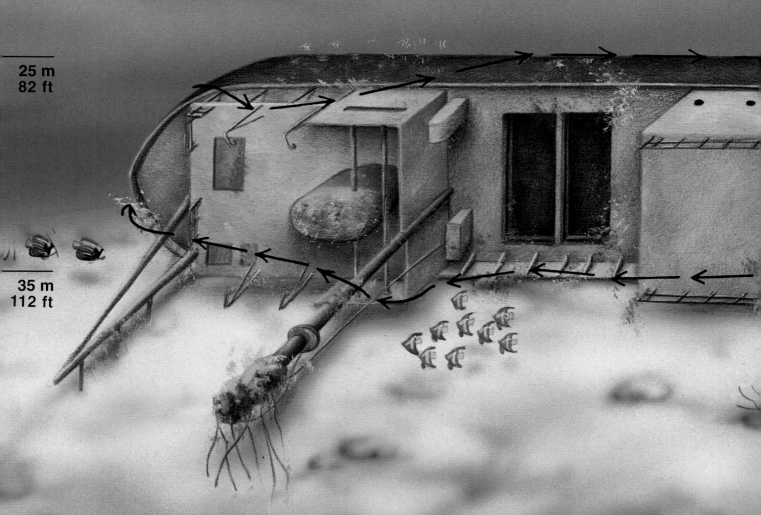

0 m
0 ft

12 m
40 ft

25 m
82 ft

35 m
112 ft

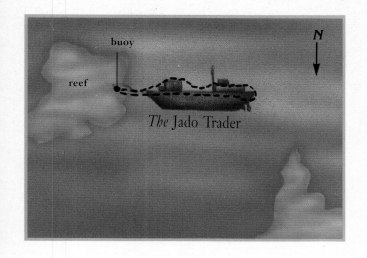

buoy

reef

*The* Jado Trader

N

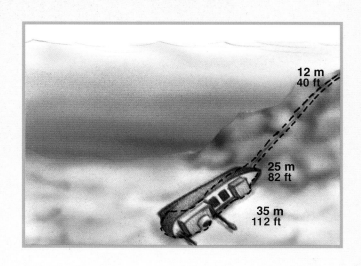

12 m
40 ft

25 m
82 ft

35 m
112 ft

## LOCATION

The *Jado Trader*, abandoned by its owners for years, was scuttled in 1977 as an attraction for divers. The merchant vessel measures 230 feet (70 meters) long, and lies on its starboard side at a depth of 108 feet (33 meters). It is located almost 2 miles (over 3 kilometers) off the southeast coast of South West Caye. The prow points to a huge coral rump that rises from the sea bed to 40 feet (12 meters) below the surface.

A

B

C

D

The huge anchor chain leads from this coral rump to the wreck. After exploring the ship, you travel back along the same route and ascend by the buoy cable. Those with enough time and air can stay on the reef plateau, which is completely covered with soft corals and where you can see huge shoals of fish. The *Jado Trader* dive is suitable only for experts because of its depth, the possibility of currents, and the strict dive plan.

## THE DIVE

We start our dive following the anchor chain. There is a light to medium current and we reach the wreck along the sea bottom. Visibility is excellent, and the silhouette of the wreck already stands out against the deep blue. A group of

*A. The big cargo holds have been transformed into lairs for fish.*

*B. The old merchant vessel rests on its starboard side; abandoned by humans, it has become an ideal habitat for a large number of species.*

*C. Clear water with currents of varying strength make it possible to see most of the wreck.*

*D. The black silhouettes of groupers against the light of divers' torches.*

4 or 5 enormous groupers appears, forming a reception committee. They are regular guests at the wreck and are awaiting food brought by the dive master. There is an extraordinary wealth of fish life inside and around the wreck. Angelfish, blue surgeonfish, and hogfish are all hunting for food in the hull and there are shoals of jacks all around the superstructure. The wreck is just like the ones you see in books. Still fully intact, its hawsers remain attached to the mast, and the cargo

depth of over 98 feet (30 meters), so time passes quickly. We take another glance at the poop deck. There are schools of silversides inside the rear deck, too, and we take a last look at the enormous perch that lives in the wreck, before it disappears into the hull. For a better view of the arched poop deck, which looks more like that on a pirate ship than a merchant vessel, it is best to keep your distance from the wreck, the rudder, and the propellor. There is another buoy cable leading from this part of the

E. The ship's bridge rises up like a wall, providing a safe shadow for the big black grouper (Mycteroperca bonaci) that has claimed the vessel as its own.

F. The incrustations on the hull have transformed inanimate sheet metal into a gallery of colors that only the divers' torches can illuminate.

G. Cables and parts of the superstructure still hang from the ship's cargo masts, creating strange, contorted bundles, brightened by the organisms that have set up home on the slim supports.

E

F

cranes and masts are covered with all kinds of organisms.

We start our exploration through the cargo hatches. You should definitely bring a torch. We enter the hull, where thousands of silversides dart in the cone of light. A green moray eel over 5 feet (1.5 meters) long lives here and actually follows the divers around. The mast rising from the superstructure and the chimney stack make good photographs, especially with a diver holding a flashlight in the background. Although it is possible to go inside, it is strongly discouraged because the extremely narrow passages are obstructed by cables. We are at a

G

ship to another nearby coral block. About 33 feet (10 meters) away from the wreck of the *Jado Trader* there is a big red gorgonian that makes another great photograph. This way back to the prow takes us up along the backboard railing, to a depth of 75 feet (23 meters), which means we can save on air and take a look at the coral plateau right beneath the dive boat.

# Guanaja:
## Jim's Silver Lode

reef

**GUANAJA**

South West Caye

▼ *Jim's Silver Lode*

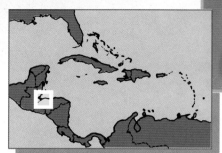

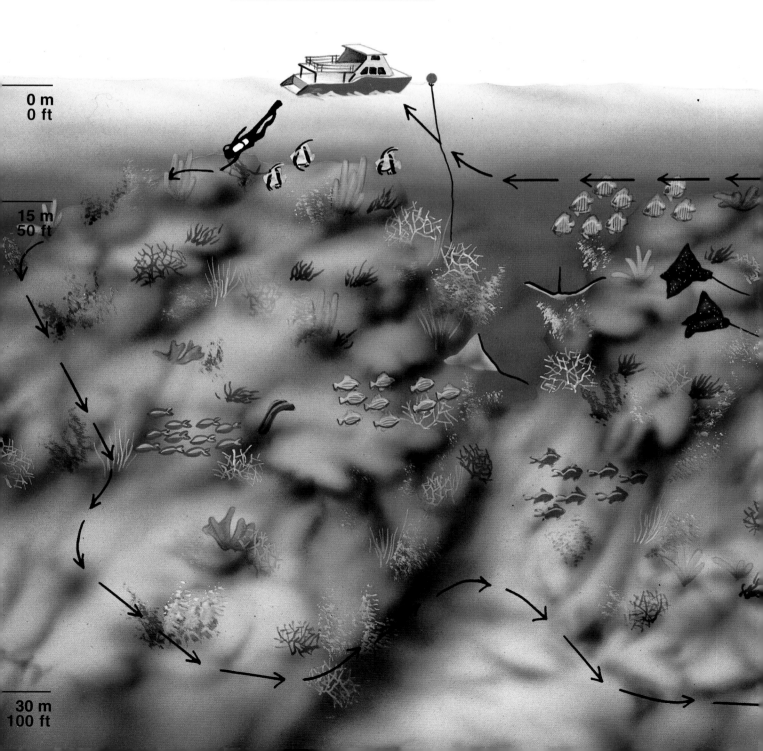

0 m
0 ft

15 m
50 ft

30 m
100 ft

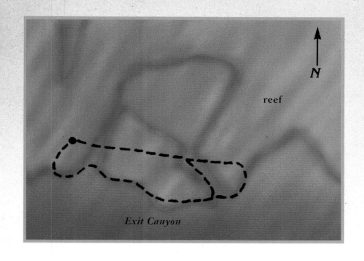

reef

N

Exit Canyon

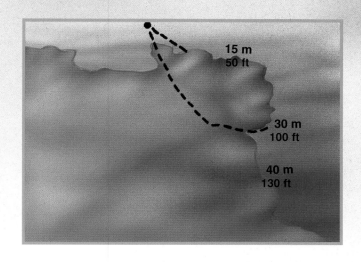

15 m
50 ft

30 m
100 ft

40 m
130 ft

## LOCATION

Jim's Silver Lode is one of the most popular dive sites around Guanaja. It is southeast of South West Caye and has a permanent buoy to moor the dive boat. The site is named for the schools of silversides found in the hollows of the drop-off. The reef's sheer wall is truly spectacular. From the edge of the reef, at about 50 feet (15 meters), the wall drops vertically for another 3,280 feet (1,000 meters); you often see very big fish here, schools of jacks or stingrays. The dive masters have created a practically

perfect circular expanse of sand right behind the reef as a fish-feeding station. The groupers here have been getting increasingly large, and seem fearless when confronted. Other inhabitants of the reef include 2 enormous morays and a big barracuda. There are groups of adult yellowtail snappers, royal triggerfish, and butterflyfish; angelfish are everywhere.

Strong currents are rare and it is always easy to get back to the buoy or dive boat. Jim's Silver Lode is a suitable site for divers of all levels of experience, though good buoyancy control is essential to swim along the drop-off. Remember that at this

point of the wall the reef plunges vertically into the deep.

## THE DIVE

There are 5 or 6 enormous groupers waiting for us immediately underneath the boat. Their interest is captured by the white food basket brought by one of the dive masters. The fish know quite well what will be waiting for them at the end of our tour, so they accompany our group for the entire dive.

Leaving the huge sandy expanse behind us, we head through a narrow

A. *The sandy sea floor winds in among the rocky walls of a long canyon.*

B. *The canyon exit stands out against the blue of the drop-off, where divers can hang in the water hundreds of meters above the sea floor.*

C. *A stunning Caribbean seascape: sea fans, hard corals, sea plumes, sponges, and colorful fish, such as the purple blackcap basslet* (Gramma melacara).

D. *A dense group of orange and yellow tube sponges* (Aplysina fistularis), *one of the most common types in the Caribbean.*

E. *This particular coral ledge provides an ideal substrate for the slim, red stick sponges and deep-water sea fans.*

F. *A black grouper* (Mycteroperca bonaci), *measuring almost 3 feet (1 meter) long.*

G. *A rare gilded grouper, called a coney* (Epinephelus fulvus). *This variety is more common in the most sheltered parts of the reef, where it stays close to the sea floor.*

H. *A green moray* (Gymnothorax funebris) *leaves its lair, a rare opportunity for any diver in open waters.*

I. *The shape of elkhorn corals* (Acropora palmata) *becomes familiar after a few dives.*

canyon filled with soft and hard coral. To keep our fins from damaging the coral, we have to swim along its widest part. Photographers and cameramen have to work with great care because rising air bubbles detach particles from the roof.

The exit opens onto the deep blue of the drop-off. Depending on the current, you can go right or left here. The sensation you experience swimming along the wall of the reef, knowing that the floor is over a thousand meters below, is indescribable. The drop-off, which starts at around 46 feet (14 meters), has very rich vegetation. Next to the forests of soft corals we encounter all kinds of sponges. From 98 feet (30 meters) we come across an increasing number of deep-sea corals—sea whip corals, for the most part, along with big reddish brown clumps of black corals. The landscape in front of us is amazing, but we want to look into the reef's hollows and crannies and underneath the outcrops. This is where the rare blackcap basslet lives. With an expert dive master, you can visit the "silver-sides crevice," a grotto 65 feet (20 meters) down packed with these silvery fish, who shine like lightning in the sun's rays. Photographers should use a very light flashgun to avoid excessive reflection from the fish. We go through a large sand shut to the sandy area and meet the groupers again. They have been joined by a large moray eel.

Lunchtime for them, at last. The dive master shares out the food with determined impartiality. You can watch the show kneeling comfortably on the sand or make a final tour of the reef surface at about 33 feet (10 meters), in the direction opposite the drop-off.

# Guanaja: Black Rocks

Black Rocks

reef

GUANAJA

10 m
30 ft

20 m
65 ft

sand tunnels

N

sand

cave

reef

Black Rocks

6 m
18 ft

10 m
30 ft

20 m
65 ft

## LOCATION

These black lavic rocks are located on the leeward side of the island, to the northeast of the little village of Mangrove Bight. The entire sea bed is volcanic in origin and has a bizarre appearance, with caves, crevices, and hollows, quite unique in the Bay Islands. The Black Rocks reef is 1.5 miles (2 kilometers) long and you can swim a long way into the many canyons and crevices. The depth of the plateau is between 3 and 20 feet (1 and 6 meters) and the sea bed itself is never deeper than 65 feet (20 meters). The water is generally clear. In this kind of transparency, the Black Rocks imbue the landscape with a unique coldness.

This site features the same species of fish as we saw at other dive sites on Guanaja, although there are not

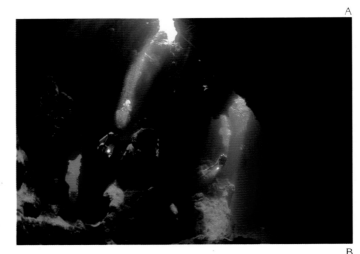

A

B

C

- D

*A. A strange landscape of caverns, canyons, and grottoes.*

*B. The volcanic origins and shadiness of the Black Rocks area prevent encrustant organisms from creating the richly colored palettes of other Caribbean sea beds.*

*C. The black volcanic rocks and the blue of the sea create cathedral-like settings.*

*D. The Black Rocks caves are not all frightening; in many places they have large openings to the sea.*

as many here as in other places. Furthermore, the geological structure of the sea bed is less suitable for coral and there is less of it. However, you will see thousands of copper sweepers in the hollows and the caves of the reef. These triangular, copper-colored fish are nocturnal and spend the entire day inside caves and crevices. Huge nurse sharks are quite common in the Black Rocks, too; this area is particularly suited to bottom dwellers. But it is the chasms and the grottoes that make this place unique—not so much the long passages, which require special care to navigate, but the fact that every 65 to 80 feet (20 to 25 meters), the roof opens up through a lateral landscape to the open sea. Depending on the weather, the sun's rays penetrate through the surface or are refracted on the corners of the reef, making a spectacular sight. Sometimes you feel as if you are inside a Gothic cathedral. Underwater photographers find a wonderful challenge in capturing these light plays. Bring a good torch.

## THE DIVE

There are no permanent buoys at the Black Rocks, and drift diving is the technique usually used. Depending on the currents, divers are dropped at one end of the reef and picked up at the other. It is very comfortable to be carried along by the current and you don't have to worry about making your way back to the boat. You can concentrate on the underwater world as you let

Now that we are in the open sea, we move along the lava wall on which soft corals and sponges grow. We stop to admire a group of nurse sharks underneath the flat outcrops. Thanks to a slight current, we have been thrifty with our air reserve and can make a short trip inside one of the volcanic caves. This passage travels over 328 feet (100 meters) into the reef and is called Sandtunnel.

*E. A dense forest dominated by the big fans of gorgonians.*

*F. During the day, the darker corners of the caves are illuminated by golden reflections from dense shoals of glassy sweepers (Pempheris schomburgki).*

yourself be pushed gently along. As soon as you enter the water, you will catch your first sight of the volcanic sea floor, a chilling sensation. On morning dives, the sun is on the reef plateau and the sheer walls are in shadow, which accentuates the effect even more. The reef is full of canyons and cavities that offer infinite routes, and we enter one of many dark passages. The cone of light from the torch shows colonies of bright yellow anemones and a carpet of red sponges, black corals, and whip corals. On the V-shaped roof of the tunnel there is a shoal of copper sweepers, their shiny bodies reflecting the light. To capture them on film, use an underwater flashgun at half or even quarter strength to avoid overexposure. Bright and in bands like lasers, the sun's rays penetrate through the opening in the ceiling. The exit is just a little way ahead, a rugged crevice through which the sunlight enters the cave.

At points, it is wide enough to accommodate a truck. Numerous side passages and exits through the roof admit the sun's rays, which reflect on the sandy floor, wrapping the whole labyrinth in a mysterious half-light. The sand tunnels are the end of our dive; we swim through a huge hole out into a sandy expanse where our dive boat is anchored.

*G. Spadefish (Chaetodipterus faber), typical inhabitants of the Caribbean, swim intermixed with some snappers at the base of the caves.*

*H. The sandy beds inside the volcanic caves are an ideal place for nurse sharks (Ginglymostoma cirratum) to make their lairs.*

# Guadeloupe and Martinique

The far-flung territories of Guadeloupe and Martinique are between the Atlantic and the Caribbean. Originally inhabited by the peace-loving Arawaks from Orinoco, the islands were later invaded by the Caribs, who were warriors and cannibals. Both islands became French colonies in 1635.

There are 2 seasons in the French Antilles: cool and dry from December to April, and humid and warm from May to November. Gales and cyclones can occur during September and October. The mountain chains on the islands make the climate particularly variable. Short tropical rain showers periodically soak the land; trade winds constantly blow from north to northeast, cooling the air and ensuring that it is never oppressive close to shore. Average air temperature varies from 77°F (25°C) in winter to 90°F (32°C) in summer. Water temperature remains constant at around 75° to 85°F (24° to 28°C). In all but a few places, dive sites in the French Antilles are accessible to everyone. There are no residential stingrays, mantas, sharks, or hump-head wrasses here, but no lack of pleasant surprises, either. Some divers have the luck to see whale sharks, tarpon, hammerhead sharks, shoals of stingrays, or barracuda as big as tree trunks. Schools of jacks have made their base at some sites, as have patrolling barracuda.

*A. A stunning aerial view of the 2 small islands known as Iles de la Petit Terre, lying southeast of the main Grande Terre island, Guadeloupe.*

*B. The beautiful island coastline is not always ideal for diving.*

A

B

## GUADELOUPE

This is actually 2 islands, Grande Terre and Basse Terre, separated by a strait called Rivière Salée. Grand Terre is a vast plateau, just over 328 feet (100 meters) above sea level. Basse Terre is very mountainous, covered with tropical vegetation. Like Martinique, Guadeloupe has a windward shore, not really suitable for

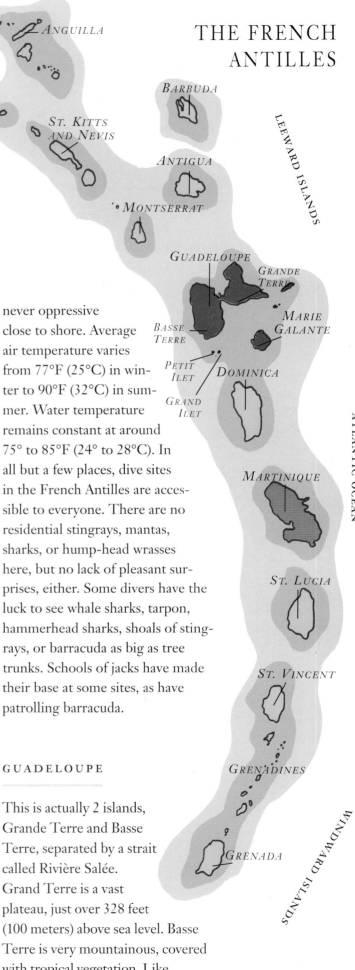

THE FRENCH ANTILLES

ANGUILLA

BARBUDA

ST. KITTS AND NEVIS

ANTIGUA

MONTSERRAT

GUADELOUPE

GRANDE TERRE

BASSE TERRE

MARIE GALANTE

PETIT ILET

GRAND ILET

DOMINICA

MARTINIQUE

ST. LUCIA

ST. VINCENT

GRENADINES

GRENADA

LEEWARD ISLANDS

ATLANTIC OCEAN

WINDWARD ISLANDS

diving, and a leeward, well-sheltered shore where the 10 best dive centers are. The dives are not particularly difficult, except for the Pâté Bank midway between Guadeloupe and Les Saintes. The most interesting sites are at depths of up to 98 feet (30 meters), with typical coralline fauna and flora and deep-water fish such as jacks, but there are no rays or sharks. With visibility nearly always excellent at depths between 33 and 130 feet (10 and 40 meters), Guadeloupe is the ideal place for beginners to dive in absolute safety. New dive centers crop up continually, especially

*C. The French Antilles have very varied countryside and rich vegetation— a gift of the rain carried by the trade winds.*

*D. Sometimes, tube sponges grow so close that they look like the pipes of an enormous organ.*

*E. The lovely white beaches in the French Antilles offer easy access to dive sites.*

*F. Yellowtail snappers (Ocyurus chrysurus) are common on the sea floors in the French Antilles.*

in the area around the Ilets Pigeons, known as the Cousteau Reserve. The reef here descends vertically to a depth of 16 to 33 feet (5 to 10 meters), at which point the sea bed becomes a rocky platform to a depth of 50 to 65 feet (15 to 20 meters), before dropping away again from 65 to 147 feet (20 to 45 meters). Each mooring buoy marks the entry for several dives.

## MARTINIQUE

Martinique's gentle leeward coast on the Caribbean side is bathed by clear waters. The windward Atlantic shore has high rocky cliffs pummeled by the sea and beaches beaten by deep-sea waves. The southern part of the island, drier and flat, has big sugarcane plantations and most of the tourist facilities. The north offers a wilder, more mountainous landscape, with dense tropical forest alternating with banana and pineapple plantations.

Unlike the Caribbean shore, the rough Atlantic coast is not very popular with divers. The northern part of the island does have some impressive underwater walls and one exceptional, very deep site— the St. Pierre wrecks, which resulted from the 1902 eruption of Mount Pelée. The humid climate and the freshwater inlets from streams greatly reduce underwater visibility. The Anses d'Arlets area in the south provides endless dive sites accessible to everyone; another renowned dive point is the even more southerly Rocher du Diamant.

One of Martinique's most extraordinary characteristics is the wealth of different sponges. They are everywhere, in a beautiful variety of species and colors: yellow organ pipes, brown drums opening up to the surface, blue trees, and opalescent vases trimmed in transparent lace.

# Guadeloupe: Jacks Reef

GUADELOUPE

Grande Terre

Basse Terre

Marie Galante

Grand Ilet

Petit Ilet — Jacks Reef

0 m
0 ft

8 m
26 ft

20 m
65 ft

23 m
70 ft

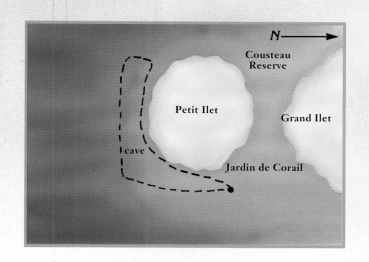

N ⟶

Cousteau
Reserve

Petit Ilet

Grand Ilet

cave

Jardin de Corail

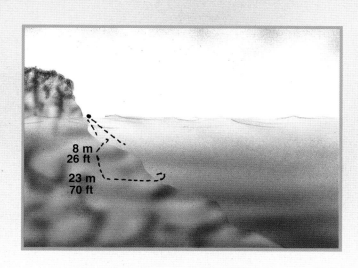

8 m
26 ft

23 m
70 ft

## LOCATION

The Jacks Reef is on the southeast side of Petit Ilet, just in front of the coast. The boat is moored at the Jardin de Corail, in the pass that separates the 2 islands. You can swim directly to the reef, following the border between the sandy bottom and the reef itself. The current can be strong, but generally the sea conditions are favorable. You will see a kind of spur on your dive; this is the best place to observe the jacks. They swim in a compact group that follows the current.

*A. Large schools of silvery jacks are a main attraction of this area.*

*B. A dense forest of sea plumes (Pseudopterogorgia sp.).*

*C. Shoals of hundreds of streamlined jacks can form an almost solid wall around a diver.*

*D. A branch from an unusual sea-rod gorgonian, many of which dominate large areas of the sea bottom. When the 8 feathered tentacles of their polyps are completely open, the gorgonians look as if they have been trimmed with bows.*

## THE DIVE

We descend to the sea bed at 20 feet (6 meters). Moving southward, we pass over the Jardin de Corail and follow the wall to a sandy expanse on the sea bed, 26 to 40 feet (8 to 12 meters) down. This is where we wait for the jacks. There can be any number from 5 to 300; it varies from day to day. Once we are on the edge of the wall, 328 feet (100 meters) from the buoy, we follow it down to 50 to 72 feet (15 to 22 meters), in a westerly direction. Fifty meters down, we see an enormous sponge, 5 feet (1.5 meters) tall and 3 feet (1 meter)

*E. Big clefts in the reef make ideal habitats for schools of blackbar soldierfish (Myripristis jacobus), who often allow divers to approach them.*

*F. The big vase sponges provide protection and temporary shelter for fish and invertebrates.*

*G. A large French angelfish (Pomacanthus paru) swims close to the reef. This elegant fish is one of the most beautiful in the Caribbean.*

*H. The less illuminated areas of the reef and the clefts along the Petit Ilet wall are home to nocturnal fish, like this squirrelfish.*

*I. Caves in the reef are home to many lobsters, which are quite happy to pose for photographs as long as the diver keeps a safe distance.*

wide. There are often porgies and Atlantic spadefish around. The dive continues along the vertical wall for 328 feet (100 meters) before turning north for 165 feet (50 meters) to the Petit Ilet wall. Sponges color the wall, which is full of crannies where lobsters, mantis prawns, porcupine fish, and morays shelter. Ascend the Petit Ilet wall on the left to get back to the mooring point to the east. Halfway back, at a depth of about 26 feet (8 meters), the wall becomes particularly colorful with many species of fish: yellowtail snappers, French grunts, goggle eyes, and more.

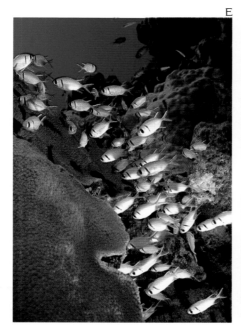

The dive continues at this depth until we reach a cave about 10 feet (3 meters) deep. We safely go in and watch the lobsters or the patterns made by the natural light. We continue for about 98 feet (30 meters), above a plateau of fire coral, before returning to the Jardin de Corail, where we wait underneath the boat and enjoy the waters.

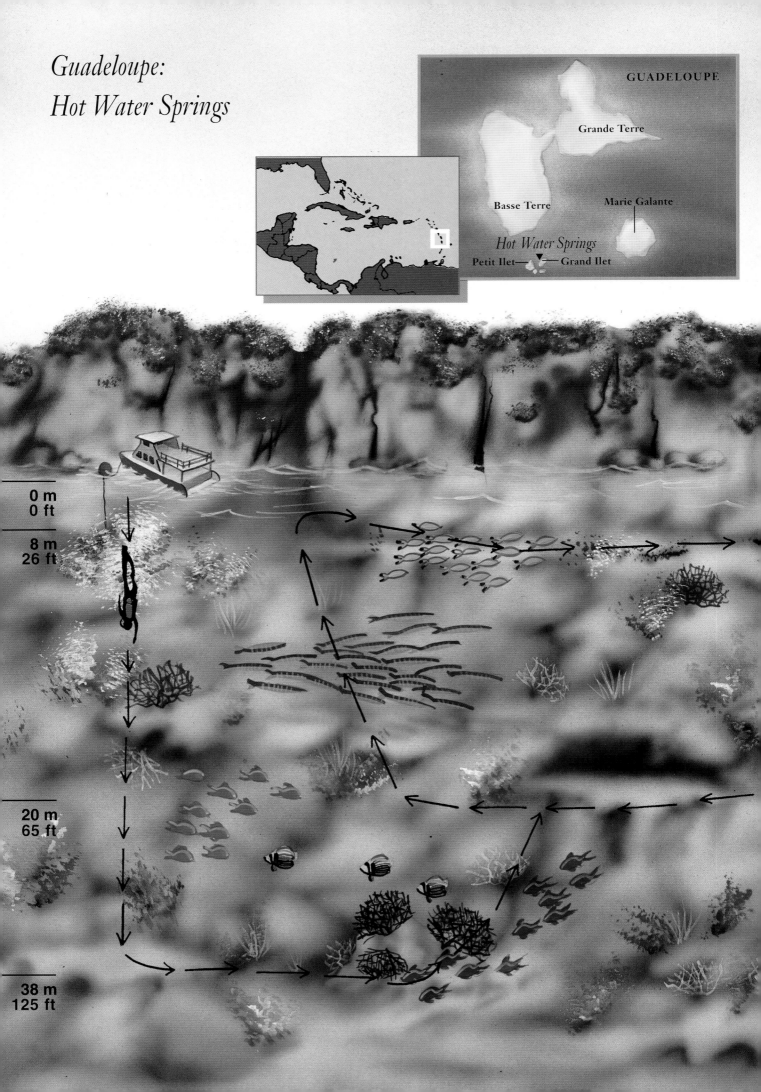

# Guadeloupe:
## Hot Water Springs

GUADELOUPE

Grande Terre

Basse Terre

Marie Galante

*Hot Water Springs*
Petit Ilet — ▼ — Grand Ilet

0 m
0 ft

8 m
26 ft

20 m
65 ft

38 m
125 ft

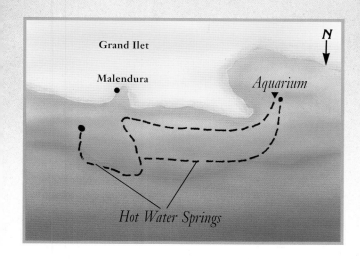

Grand Ilet

Malendura

*Aquarium*

N

Hot Water Springs

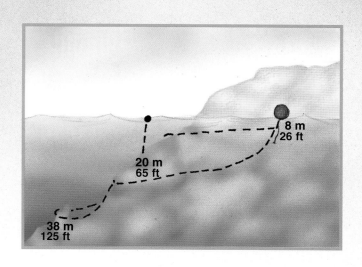

8 m
26 ft

20 m
65 ft

38 m
125 ft

## LOCATION

The Hot Water Springs are near the middle of the north side of Grand Ilet. Sometimes there is a light current parallel to the shore, but it doesn't trouble divers. Expert divers can drop just in front of the springs and, at the end of the dive, swim back to the boat moored at the Aquarium. Beginners can start the dive from the Aquarium and swim there and back. More experienced divers can do a drift-dive in the current.

## THE DIVE

We moor the boat at Grand Ilet, in the Cousteau Reserve at Malendura, Basse Terre. We enter the water at the marker buoy of the Aquarium, 16 feet (5 meters) deep, then follow the edge of the wall at a depth of 65 feet (20 meters) for about 492 feet (150 meters) east to a tiny cavity in the wall, with a small sand bath almost 75 feet (23 meters) deep. We see the scrolls and spirals made by the hot fresh water (it will burn your fingers) as it filters through the rock and sand. Then we descend to

*A. These sea plumes sway in the currents, allowing their polyps to feed and oxygenate.*

*B. A large shoal of several kinds of grunts and snappers moves along the sea bed around the Hot Water Springs, looking for food and warmth.*

*C. A combination of sponges and feather stars is often seen on parts of the sea bed with continuous currents; even weak currents provide both species with an ideal habitat.*

*D. Some parts of the Grand Ilet reef are so rich in underwater life that a diver, whether his passion is photography or nature, could use an entire air tank at one point.*

*E. A school of jacks catches both the natural light and the camera's flash to create a silvery band in the water.*

a depth of 125 feet (38 meters), to a small white beach that is blackened where the hot water comes out. Sixty-five feet (20 meters) west is a clump of big black gorgonians and a magnificent coral outcrop. Seventy-five feet (23 meters) up at the hot water spring, there are lots of fish looking for food and warmth, including jacks and barracudas. Up at 40 feet (20 to 12 meters) deep is a platform that is traversed south for 165 feet (50 meters) to the edge of Grand Ilet, where the sea bed has large fissures rich in sea life. We continue west for 592 feet (150 meters),

making our way back to the boat. During this crossing, at depths of 26 to 16 feet (8 to 5 meters), there is plenty to see and always some surprises. Finally, we arrive at the Aquarium with its coralline masses eaten away by blue surgeonfish. We wait here quite safely, watching the prawns, damselfish, butterflyfish, and boxfish as they dawdle in the coral. There are often filefish, too, which are accompanied by the dancing Creole wrasses *(Clepticus parrae).*

*F. Several different wrasse and serranid species swim together among the gorgonian fans, looking for food.*

*G. The stoplight parrotfish* (Sparisoma viride) *is one of the most common parrotfish species. It undergoes a considerable color change over the course of its life. This one's colors indicate that its sex is changing from female to male.*

*H. A large trunkfish* (Lactophrys trigonus), *easily identified by its unusual shape and the hump on its back. It approaches the reef in search of food.*

*I. French grunts* (Haemulon flavolineatum) *like to stay inactive for long periods of time in sheltered, shady parts of the reef.*

*J. A spotfin butterfly-fish* (Chaetodon ocellatus) *can be identified by the dark band, which hides the position of its eyes from predators.*

# Martinique: Pointe Burgos

MARTINIQUE

Mt. Pelée

Saint-Pierre

Fort-de-France

Pointe Burgos

0 m
0 ft

10 m
30 ft

20 m
65 ft

30 m
100 ft

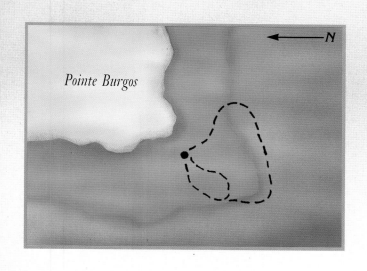

*Pointe Burgos*

N

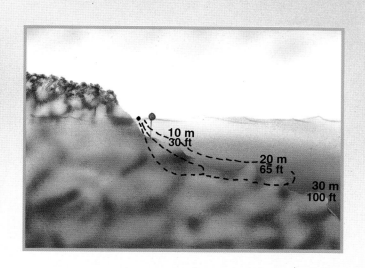

10 m
30 ft

20 m
65 ft

30 m
100 ft

## LOCATION

Pointe Burgos is famous for its resident school of Atlantic spadefish. The dive site is easy, ideal for beginners. The usual absence of current ensures good visibility. Pointe Burgos is right after Pointe Lezarde, almost opposite the Rocher du Diamant. There is a permanent mooring at 26 feet (8 meters), about 165 feet (50 meters) offshore.

*A. A small school of gray snappers (Lutjanus griseus) seeks protection at the base of a gigantic hard coral.*

## THE DIVE

At 33 to 40 feet (10 to 12 meters), the angle of the sea bed increases and there is a tongue of rock, covered in fissures, that descends to 65 feet (20 meters). The first part makes a more than adequate dive: the area is home to schools of snappers the locals call "sorbes" and "gorettes" (French grunts), as well as a multitude of reef fish—sergeant majors, trumpetfish, and damselfish. There are also masses of sponges of all shapes and colors, one of the main attractions of diving in Martinique. If you descend to a depth of 82 to 98 feet (25 to 30 meters), you can continue out to sea, where a coral reef forms a peak that rises back up to a depth of 72 to 75 feet (22 to 23 meters). You can run into jacks, wrasses, and splendid schools of spadefish here. Continue

*B. The double spiral tuft is characteristic of the Christmas tree worm (Spirobranchus giganteus), which keeps its calcareous tube hidden in the coral.*

*C. A Creole wrasse (Clepticus parrae) swims close to a big sponge, which is sheltering a large, dark crinoid.*

*D. Crinoids often choose large vase sponges as shelters, and feed by extending their thin, feathered branches.*

*E. A large shoal of jacks with a single barracuda, swimming in the sun's filtered rays.*

*F. The sergeant major (Abudefduf saxatilis), a pomacentrid, is among the least shy of all fish and often approaches divers of its own accord.*

*G. Two barracuda swim close to the surface on Pointe Burgos.*

*H. This Atlantic spadefish (Chaetodipterus faber) swims along the base of the wall, where the polyps of small, solitary hard corals grow like flowers.*

*I. The silhouette of a yellowtail snapper (Ocyurus chrysurus) appears in the blue.*

downward to 108 feet (33 meters) and head south to an enormous wall that plunges from 115 to 328 feet (35 to 100 meters). Here the big predators pass; you can see rays or schools of jacks. There has even been a sighting of a whale shark. Sometimes, stingrays hide under the sediment on the sea bed. The face of the underwater wall itself is carpeted with *Montipora foliosa* corals, huge coral flowers with petals stretched out to the sun. Stop at 10 to 13 feet (3 to 4 meters) on the way back to the boat, to look along the sea bed where small grottoes alternate with sandy spaces. The light filtering through the surface of the water gives you the impression of being in an underwater garden inhabited by snappers and damselfish, periodically disturbed by a large barracuda.

F

G

E

H

I

# Martinique:
## Rocher du Diamant

MARTINIQUE

Mt. Pelée

Saint-Pierre

Fort-de-France

*Rocher du Diamant*

0 m
0 ft

20 m
65 ft

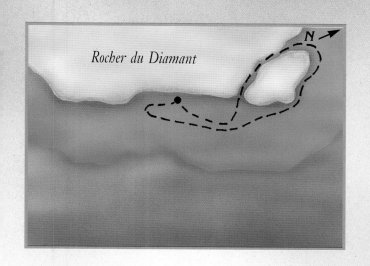

*Rocher du Diamant*

N

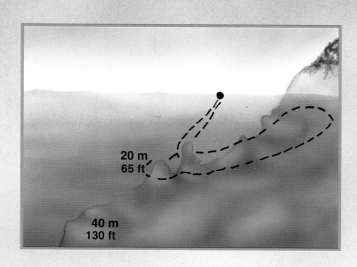

20 m
65 ft

40 m
130 ft

## LOCATION

This dive promises to be unforgettable but is reserved for those with some experience. The mooring is south-southeast of Rocher du Diamant at a depth of 60 feet (18 meters). Diving is best in the morning; the deep water has greater light then, and it is the best time to see passing ocean fish.

## THE DIVE

You will be accompanied on the long descent to the sea bed by yellowtail snappers and jacks. Keep a constant depth of 60 feet (18 meters) and move off parallel to Rocher du Diamant. The first stop is a cavern in the

*A. The huge outline of the Rocher du Diamant emerges from the waves like a fortress, with walls that plunge down to 196 feet (60 meters).*

*B. A school of blackbar soldierfish (Myripristis jacobus) swims close to a big cleft in the rock.*

*C. A group of horse-eye jacks (Caranx latus) illuminate the blue depths surrounding the Rocher du Diamant with their silvery bodies.*

*D. Sponges, gorgonians, and hard corals seem to grow in a chaotic jumble; actually, they are competing with one another for territory.*

*E. Bream swarm around a diver who is busy filming a group of sponges. The sponges are growing above a colony of pencil coral (Madracis mirabilis) with short, dense branches.*

direction of Rocher du Diamant, where huge brown gorgonian sea fans stretch their branches into the current and where numerous lobsters poke their antennae out of their dens. Farther away, a large ravine about 40 feet (12 meters) deep opens up into an underwater cathedral that runs for 165 feet (50 meters). Safe from any outside aggression, purple corals, white gorgonians, and an infinite number of colored sponges thrive on the walls. At the end of the ravine, you swim out into the turquoise waters of the open sea once more. The way back to the boat is around the ravine and up from 40 feet (12 meters) to the surface along a vertical wall punctuated with small caves, fissures, and plunging voids. Triggerfish, damselfish, wrasses—every possible species is present.

Expert scuba divers can do a deeper version of the same dive. A quiet descent out to the open sea leads to a magnificent vertical wall that plunges from 130 to 196 feet (40 to 60 meters). It is full of deep caves that lead dangerously into the rock. The dive continues through a chimney up to the top of the wall. With luck, this dive can be a fascinating experience; you can see

*F. A small red hind* (Epinephelus guttatus) *looks curiously out of a crevice on the sea floor.*

*G. The longspine squirrelfish* (Holocentrus rufus) *tends to spend the daylight hours in darker parts of the reef.*

*H. Atlantic spotted dolphins* (Stenelle frontalis) *are a fairly common sight in the waters around the Rocher du Diamant. This site is also a point of passage for many big pelagic fish.*

*I. A large lobster surprised in front of its lair at the base of the reef. Some Caribbean lobsters migrate long distances in the mating season.*

*J. The sea around the Rocher du Diamant is full of currents, ideal for sighting spotted eagle rays* (Aetobatus narinari).

hammerhead sharks or—even more exceptional—whale sharks. In fact, the Rocher du Diamant is one of the places where you are most likely to see the big fish. You may also see big mammals: in March and April, humpback and sperm whales swim near the rock, and a school of dolphins plies the island's leeward coast all year round. White-tailed eagles and tropical birds sweep the length and breadth of the skies.

# THE DUTCH ANTILLES
## *Curaçao*

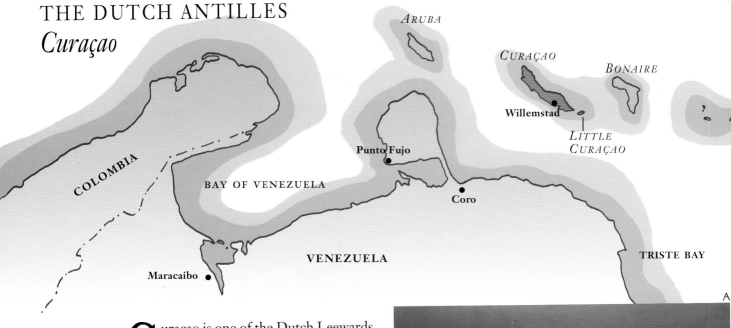

*A. Curaçao's coral platform is dominated by gorgonians of all types and sizes. Candelabra and sea-rod gorgonians grow alongside the classic fans.*

Curaçao is one of the Dutch Leewards, which are also known as the ABC islands (Aruba, Bonaire, Curaçao). Just 37 miles (60 kilometers) from Venezuela, it has a total area of 171 square miles (444 square kilometers), making it the biggest of the Dutch Antilles. Southwest of Curaçao lies Little Curaçao, an uninhabited island 1.5 miles (2.5 kilometers) long, with a lighthouse. Curaçao's climate is typically tropical. The sun shines virtually all the time and the northeast trade winds blow all year round, ensuring a little cool relief. The mean annual temperature is 81°F (27.5°C).

### HISTORY

The island was discovered in 1499 by Alonso de Ojeda, a sublieutenant traveling with Columbus. It was inhabited by the tall Arawak Indians, and, for this reason, the Spaniards called it Isla de Los Gigantes. Less than 20 years later, the name Curaçao appeared for the first time on a Portuguese map, but even now the origin of the name is obscure. The most credible theory is that the Spaniards renamed the island *Curazon* ("heart").

The island belonged to the Spanish crown until 1634, when it was taken by the Dutch (although the British and French continually tried to conquer it). In 1954 the island gained independence from the Kingdom of the Netherlands. The island's history can still be seen in the remaining colonial-era fortifications, plantation houses that belonged to the Dutch colonists,

*B. The side of this spotted trunkfish* (Lactophrys bicaudalis) *bears the marks of a recent fight.*

and caves containing paintings by the native Arawaks.

Since the 1970s, tourism has been one of the main pillars of the Antillean economy. Along the southern coast there are large modern hotels, and the sea is always calm—unlike the northern coast, which is battered by huge, wild waves. The St. Elisabeth Gasthuis, with 800 beds, is the most modern hotel in the Caribbean. Curaçao has a modern airport and an excellent infrastructure, evidence of the old colonial powers and

E

*C. The lagoons of Little Curaçao are home to a large number of turtles, who appreciate the calm waters and plentiful food.*

*D. A trumpetfish* (Aulostomus maculatus) *exploits its elongated form to hide among the sponges and gorgonians.*

C

F

D

a reminder that, even in the heart of the tropics, this is a European island. There is a wide range of good restaurants: in addition to local cuisine, you can get European, Chinese, and Italian food. February is carnival month; for 3 entire days, the island's inhabitants let themselves go wild.

The island has facilities for all kinds of sport: golf, horse riding, squash, tennis, fishing, cycling, fitness, jet skiing, water skiing, sailing, surfing, water wheeling, snorkeling, and, of course, diving. There is a modern decompression chamber for underwater accidents and a 24-hour casualty center.

*E. The rounded silhouette and striped pattern of the Atlantic spadefish* (Chaetodipterus faber) *make it easy to identify.*

*F. In some places, French grunts* (Haemulon flavolineatum) *accumulate in such numbers that they make a colorful curtain, totally concealing the reef.*

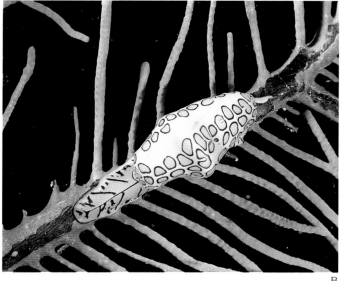

## LITTLE CURAÇAO: A DIVING PARADISE

The dive sites on this island are untouched and magical; it also boasts the most beautiful beach in all of Curaçao. All the dive centers organize day trips to this inhabited island less than .5 square mile (1 square kilometer) in size. You can arrive by helicopter, if you like, and do the return journey by boat. When you arrive, you will notice the lighthouse

in the middle of the island; it offers a splendid view from the lantern.

Apart from a single palm, the island is almost completely without vegetation. But the island was not always so barren. The hills were once covered with green meadows, trees, and plants on which Dutch horses grazed. Around 1880, however, an Englishman got permission to mine the deep layer of phosphate created by fermented manure. The mining soon transformed this splendid island into a dry, desolate surface.

The reef off the coast of Little Curaçao is virtually intact, home to enormous fan corals and gorgonians. The waters are filled with the wrecks

*A. A unique mollusk known as a flamingo tongue (Cyphoma gibbosum), feeding on gorgonian polyps.*

*B. A grouper (Cephalopholis fulva) in one typical color scheme.*

*C. Two gray angelfish (Pomacanthus arcuatus) mirror each other, showing off their bluebordered fins and yellow pectorals.*

*D. In the Seaquarium Animal Encounter, you can feed sharks under the careful eye of an expert dive master.*

*E. The compact petrified fans of the common Gorgonia ventalina can reach a height of 6.5 feet (2 meters).*

*F. The rich underwater life of Curaçao, where sponges, gorgonians, hard corals, and sea plumes colonize every rock formation.*

*G. These old coral ramifications, encrusted with sponges and other organisms, provide shelter to grunts (Haemulon sp.) and snappers (Lutjanus sp.).*

of ships. On the reef behind the navigation light, there is the rusty wreck of the Dutch oil tanker *Bianca Maria Guidesman*, which got stuck on the reef and is now being inexorably eaten by rust. The big holes in the bows and amidships make it particularly interesting for photographers. About halfway along the beach is an eighteenth-century cannon from the Dutch East India Company. The lagoon is scattered with anchors and chains from the ships that moored here around 300 years ago.

A great number of turtles swim the lagoon, and several times a year, huge whales approach the island and can be seen from the edge of the ledge. Numerous whale species pass in the winter, including the sperm and the humpback. Every year, the marine biology research institute at Carmabi receives notice of at least 5 killer whale sightings.

## DIVING IN CURAÇAO

With over 100 dive sites, Curaçao can be included in a list of the most beautiful dive meccas in the Caribbean. All of the island's dive sites are on the south coast; trade winds make the north coast too rough. There are 3 different zones: the section from Westpunt to the Kaap St. Marie lighthouse, called Banda Abao; the Centraal Curaçao dive area between Bullenbaai and the Princess Beach Hotel; and the Curaçao Underwater Park, which runs from the Princess Beach Hotel to Oostpunt.

There are moorings in the underwater reserve and at Banda Abao to protect the splendid reef. The reef is close to the coast and the Centraal Curaçao dive sites can be reached by car. The coast shelves gently into quite shallow water, and the drop-off starts just 165 to 328 feet

F

G

(50 to 100 meters) from the coast, plunging for hundreds of meters in several points. It is a typical coral barrier reef, with a wide variety of hard and soft corals, gorgonians, big sponges, shallow- and deep-water fish, and many species of invertebrates. Every dive promises something new and unexpected— a shoal of Atlantic tarpon or a solitary hammerhead shark.

There are some really beautiful wrecks to visit on Curaçao, the biggest of which is the *Superior Producer* at Willemstad. The Seaquarium has the wreck of the Dutch steamer SS *Orange Nassau*. The little *Towboat* rests in the Caracasbaai area. This

wreck is covered with splendid vegetation and must rank as one of the most beautiful in the Caribbean. Closer to the Princess Beach Hotel, the wreck of the tug *Saba* lies in relatively shallow waters near the Car Pile, a heap of 1950s auto carcasses. There are magnificent anchors of old ships to be seen all over.

In Curaçao, you can either boat dive or enter straight from the shore. There are many well-organized dive centers, and practically every hotel has its own operation. They all belong to the DCOA, the association of all Curaçao dive schools. Underwater harpoon fishing is absolutely forbidden throughout the island.

Curaçao: Mushroom Forest

Westpunt
CURAÇAO
Santa Marta Baai
Mushroom Forest
Willemstad
Punt Kanon

0 m
0 ft

10 m
30 ft

15 m
50 ft

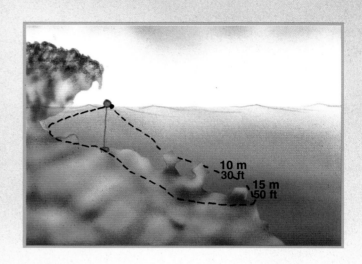

A

B

C

F

Mushroom Forest is not too far from the Coral Cliff Hotel at Banda Abao, on the west side of the island. It is one of the most bizarre and beautiful sites I have ever explored, a bay with mushroom-shaped coral banks several meters high. How and why this type of coral developed here is still a mystery. A wide variety of fish and other marine animals live among the coral banks and it is not unusual to meet turtles.

*A. A short distance from the surface, the sea bed is characterized by mushroom-shaped hard coral formations. The "stalks" have probably been eroded by drilling sponges.*

*B. Colonies of boulder star coral* (Montastrea) *cover large parts of the sea bed, resembling petrified waterfalls.*

*C. The Mushroom Forest is dominated by dome-shaped coral formations that cover the surrounding rocks.*

*D. Seen from above in natural light, the Mushroom Forest looks like a valley with petrified vegetation.*

*E. The foureye butterflyfish* (Chaetodon capistratus) *derives its name from the 2 ocellar marks on the flanks of young specimens.*

*F. It is not known why these coral formations are so common in this particular zone.*

D

E

## THE DIVE

We swim about 328 feet (100 meters) from the mooring buoy to the open sea, where the water starts to get deep and the biggest mushrooms appear. The mushroom-shaped coral banks dominate the scene and we see big beaker corals and numerous colorful fish. Spiny lobsters and morays hide underneath the coral. Little saber-toothed blennies, which hide in the empty homes of several kinds of worms, swim in and out of the brain coral's labyrinth. The depth here is between 33 and 50 feet

(10 and 15 meters). At the end of the dive, we come back to the mooring buoy and swim toward the coast, where we find a cave. It is quite easy to enter and admire the yellow tube corals on the ceiling and the numerous little glassfish that swim close to the rocks. There are spiny lobsters and several kinds of prawns living there permanently, too. Do not go in unless you brought your torch!

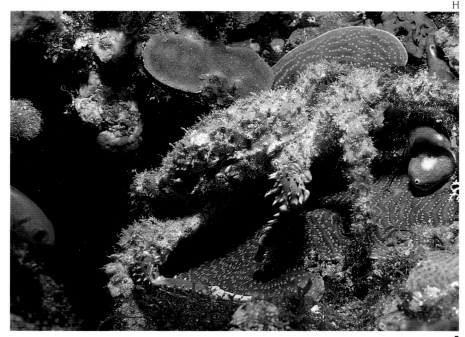

*G. A gigantic dome-like colony of brain coral (Diploria labyrinthiformis). Deep ridges protect the polyps and form an intricate design on the surface.*
*H. A strange crab with spines and bristles camouflages itself among the coral that encrusts the sea bed.*

*I. A fairy basslet (Gramma loreto). The males hold the eggs in their mouths until hatching time.*

*J. A spotted moray (Gymnothorax moringa) peers out of its lair. It stays hidden inside all day, coming out at night to hunt.*

# Curaçao:
## *The* Superior Producer S.A.

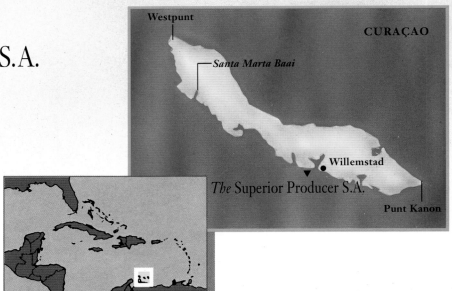

Westpunt

CURAÇAO

*Santa Marta Baai*

Willemstad

*The* Superior Producer S.A.

Punt Kanon

0 m
0 ft

24 m
80 ft

30 m
100 ft

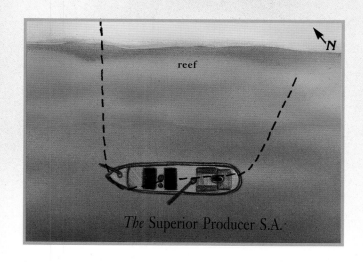

reef

*The* Superior Producer S.A.

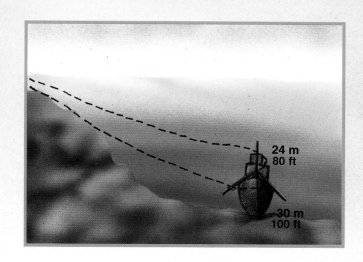

24 m
80 ft

30 m
100 ft

*A. The sinking of the* Superior Producer S.A. *Here she is surrounded by several ships that came to her aid and tried to refloat her.*

*B. Members of the crew clustered on the port side of the sinking ship.*

*C. The* Superior Producer S.A. *in its final resting place.*

*D. The front end of the ship, like the whole wreck, is covered in splendid tube corals that open in the late afternoon and at night.*

*E. The bows and part of the bridge and superstructure, seen from above.*

*F. This dramatic image clearly shows the wreck and its broken cargo mast.*

*G. The holds of the* Superior Producer S.A. *were piled high with bales of clothes, sheets, blankets, whisky, and more when she sank.*

*H. The ship has become an ideal substrate for hundreds of colorful organisms that brighten her corroded metal.*

A

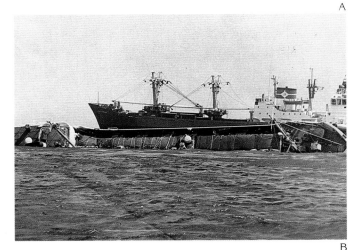

B

C

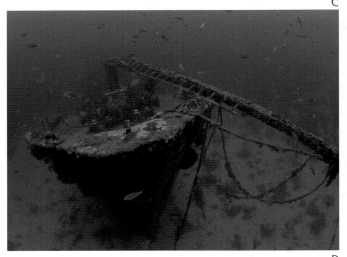

D

## LOCATION

Diving on the *Superior Producer S.A.* is easy; boat dives are scheduled a few times a week by various Curaçao dive centers. It is especially thrilling to dive from the helicopter that leaves from the platform opposite the Eden Roc Divecenter.

Dives onto the wreck can be made from shore as well. The ship lies on the east side of the water factory, so take the road that leads to the waterfront. You can stop at the mangrove forest, which has a clearing where you can leave the car.

E

## HISTORY

The *Superior Producer S.A.* was built in the Netherlands by Kramer and Booy N.V. of Spaarndam, for Moerman of Rotterdam; it was originally named *Andromeda*. The ship was launched on August 10, 1957, passed its sea trials on November 8, and was then registered. It is 162 feet (49.5 meters) long and 26 feet (8 meters) wide. Its 500-horsepower, 6-cylinder engine could haul it to a top speed of 10 knots.

In 1962, the ship was sold to L. Remeeus N.V., who changed its name to *Superior Producer*. In 1973, it was sold to the Pan-Ven Line S.A. and renamed *Superior Producer S.A.* It continued to sail for this company until it sank in front of Willemstad harbor on September 30, 1977. The small merchant vessel sailed into the port of Willemstad, but was heading for the Isla de Margaritha in Venezuela. Although it was already overloaded, more cargo was packed in at Curaçao. The bridges and holds were piled high with bales of clothes, sheets, blankets, whisky, and Alkolada Glacial, the famous Curaçao perfume. When it left port on September 30, 1977, the sea was quite strong—even for Curaçao, where they are used to extremely violent winds. The ship had not even left port when the pilot disembarked and the wind started to push it around. At the first big wave, *Superior Producer S.A.* capsized. It continued to float and other ships rushed to tow it away from the channel. The crew stayed on board while the ship started to tilt dangerously. Unsuccessful attempts were made to float the ship by removing part of the cargo, but it was futile. At 3:30 P.M., the ship disappeared into the waves and sank in a few minutes. The 10 crew members had to swim 656 feet (200 meters) to reach the shore safely. Only a few hours later, divers put lines on the ship, which was blocking access to the harbor, and it was towed 1,640 feet (500 meters) west toward the desalination plant. These divers spread the news about the easy-to-reach wreck, which was lying on its keel on the sea bed at a depth of 98 feet (30 meters), only 656 feet (200 meters) from the coast. Many keen divers on Curaçao took an interest in it and the race to the wreck was on.

F

G

## THE DIVE

We enter the water from the shore near some concrete blocks and swim on the surface straight out toward the drop-off. After about 328 feet (100 meters) we reach the edge of the reef and dive down, following the slope, to see the wreck about 165 feet (50 meters) from the reef. It rests on its keel at 98 feet (30 meters), parallel to and not far from the coral reef, covered with magnificent corals. During the day, the corals are closed, but after twilight the covering of tube corals

transforms the reef into a yellow garden. The stairway behind the bridge makes a wonderful background—but while I am looking for the best position, something brushes my shoulders. A great barracuda at least 5 feet (1.5 meters) long is swimming around the mast! It lets me approach, but the camera makes it look very small despite my powerful lens. In the half light of the bridge, I find a big school of longspine squirrelfish *(Holocentrus rufus)*. Nothing at all remains of the ship's furnishings. I look through the open portholes into the empty

H

holds at the front end of the boat. The front loading bays with a school of colorful Creole wrasse *(Clepticus parrae)* make a great picture. The depth—the bridge is at 82 feet (25 meters)—means that time is almost up. Skimming over the sandy bottom, I turn toward the reef and from there to the shore. Be aware of the current and the waves. Normally, there are breaking waves at this dive site and you must be careful entering and leaving the water. Do not spend too much time floating on the surface because the current can take you far from the wreck.

# THE FISH OF THE CARIBBEAN

The Caribbean runs along the tropical coastlines of the American continents and continues through the archipelago bounded by the Caribbean Sea on the inside and the Atlantic Ocean on the outside. This band of islands is around 497 miles (800 kilometers) wide and almost 1,242 miles (2,000 kilometers) long. The total area is modest when compared to the Pacific, where a single reef—the Australian Great Barrier Reef—alone takes up an area only slightly smaller. However, this is one of the richest coral areas in the Atlantic, with more than 600 species of fish and almost 100 different corals. Most of these originated in relatively recent times (10 to 15 years ago), when the land that today forms Central America rose up and closed off all links to the Pacific. This certainly reduced the number of species and families, but it also permitted the evolution of unique populations.

The Caribbean is dominated by the east-to-west Caribbean current and by a coastal countercurrent, which affect each other reciprocally and create numerous internal vortices. This is of notable importance to the marine life: the complex current transports countless larvae of a huge variety of animals from one area to another, contributing to their diffusion and giving a reasonably uniform character to the whole of the Caribbean. Even on their very first dive, visitors will notice that the waters are dominated by sponges and sea fans that take the place of the alcyonarians in the Red Sea and in Indo-Pacific waters.

The Caribbean coral banks stretch from Florida to the Bahamas and on to Venezuela. A huge platform east of Florida stretches right to the Bahamas, which incorporates more than 3,000 islands, cays, and reefs, creating one of the largest barriers in the Atlantic. The coral continues in the reefs off the long arc of islands from Cuba to Aruba. The coral barrier that runs parallel to the coast of Belize is 250 miles (402 kilometers) long and is considered the second most important in the world, after Australia's Great Barrier Reef. "Blue holes" are typical of this area; they are the remains of underwater caves whose vaults have collapsed, leaving broad abysses of an intense blue.

Diving in the Caribbean shows you a strange underwater world, where, alongside corals (not unlike those of the Indo-Pacific) you will find huge sponges in incredible shapes and colors. Shaped like huge elephant ears, barrels, stove pipes, or elegant candelabras, and in shades of pink, red, or yellow, they grow to sizes so enormous that they can hide one diver from another. In view of their size, it comes as no surprise that they attract swarms of rays, bream, and damselfish. Sand stars, anemones, worms, crustaceans, and fish (gobies and blennies) make their homes in the corals' big oscula. Trumpetfish or scorpionfish lie in ambush in the shadows of the sponges, sometimes joined by the brightly colored fairy basslets (Gramma loreto), easily recognized by their fluorescent yellow-and-fuchsia coloring.

The walls of the Caribbean reefs also have forests of gorgonians growing on them, from those with a regular pattern of ramifications—the fans of the Venuses, Gorgonia flabellum—to the much larger and more irregular ones—the Gorgonia ventalina, which can grow to a height of 6.5 feet (2 meters). Mixed with them, and gradually becoming dominant as the depth increases, are the feathery, more fragile black corals.

Depending on the reef's position, its walls open up either into deep channels or into the open sea. The sea bed is in each case intricate, full of holes and fissures that are home to numerous leopard, striped, and green morays (the last of these is particular abundant in the Caribbean). There are plenty of groupers in these dens, too: red ones (Cephalopholis fulva), striped ones (Epinephelus striatus—better known as the Nassau grouper—which can change color very fast to reflect its mood), and the gigantic Epinephelus itajar, unchallenged lords of the reef and of submerged wrecks. They are visible from afar thanks to the transparency of the water and their large size, frequently well over 6.5 feet (2 meters).

Less fearsome shade lovers are squirrelfish, soldierfish, and huge shoals of glassfish, whose scales reflect any light that enters the caves. Manta rays, eagle rays, and the big stingrays live on the sandy bottoms. There is a regular sequence of corals, rocks, sand, and underwater meadows. For the most part, the fish families found in this part of the Atlantic will be familiar to anyone who has already dived in coral seas, but there is no lack of opportunities for interesting encounters and comparisons. There is much more life in these clearings and channels than might at first appear.

Everyone will be enchanted by the slow-moving grace of the French angelfish *(Pomacanthus paru)* or the gray angelfish *(Pomacanthus arcuatus)*. These can grow up to 20 inches (50 centimeters) long and seem to have no fear of divers, approaching humans spontaneously. The tranquil gait of these fish is in contrast with the rapid movements of butterflyfish—such as *Chaetodon capistratus,* perhaps the commonest fish in the area. This fish can be identified by the ocellar marking near the tail (2 marks on young fish, hence the name "foureye butterflyfish"). The *Chaetodon aculeatus,* or long-nosed butterflyfish, is much less commonly seen, since it prefers the deep reefs. It is built perfectly for swimming in the tightest of coral fissures, where it searches for invertebrates to feed on. Wherever you dive, you will find the brightly colored *Labridae* with their classic darting movement, constantly in search of food. You will have no difficulty spotting the crested porkfish *(Lachnolaimus maximus),* looking rather bedraggled thanks to the long rays along its spine. The *Thalassoma bifasciatum,* which carry out their courting rituals close to the surface during the early hours of the afternoon, are also common.

But not all Caribbean fish live alone or in pairs. There are fish that live in shoals, including the many varieties of snapper and the ubiquitous French grunt, which join together in hundreds to form lively yellow-and-blue proces-

sions. Groups of big tarpons, each over 6.5 feet (2 meters) long, can make an expedition to explore an old jetty memorable even if they are the only fish you see. They have a habit of taking up permanent residence in one place, and sometimes become a fixture at a dive site. The jacks and darting barracuda are always forming silver walls—walls that suddenly open up to give way to sharks, even hammerheads.

Finally, a word of advice for the adventurous. Be sure to take the opportunity, between dives, to visit a lagoon surrounded by mangroves. This unique environment, a halfway house between land and sea, has considerable importance in the Caribbean. The water between the mangrove roots provides a breeding ground for an enormous number of species. Among sponges of all colors you can see oysters, crabs, and jellyfish swimming upside-down. Young barracuda, in training for life in more dangerous waters, chase the young of numerous other species here, from angelfish and parrotfish to butterflyfish and ray's bream.

## CARCHARHINIDAE FAMILY

### Tiger shark
*Galeocerdo cuvieri*

◀

Short, wide nose; upper lobe of caudal fin larger than lower. Blue-gray coloring, with dark vertical bars more visible in the young. Extremely dangerous and often found in coastal, even brackish, waters. Seen along outer reef walls and offshore barriers. Grows up to 18 feet (5.5 meters) in length. Found in all the circumtropical seas.

### Bull shark
*Carcharhinus leucas*

Big body; short, rounded nose; small eyes; upper lobe of caudal fin larger than lower. Brown-gray on the back; lighter on the belly. Lives in shallow coastal waters and close to reefs; considered dangerous. Grows up to 11.5 feet (3.5 meters) in length. Found in circumtropical waters.

## GINGLYMOSTOMATIDAE FAMILY

### Nurse shark
*Ginglymostoma cirratum*

Straight body flattened along the belly; close-set dorsal fins; small mouth with two short barbels on underside of head. Yellow-gray coloring. Lives on sandy sea beds between reefs, sheltered by big corals and caves. Grows up to 14 feet (4 meters) in length. Found from Rhode Island to Brazil.

## DASYATIDAE FAMILY

### Southern stingray
*Dasyatis americana*

Lozenge-shaped body, more or less pronounced; pointed nose; slightly pointed pectoral fins. A line of tubercles runs down the center of the back; a long sharp spine in the front half of the tail. Tends to bury itself in the sand when resting on the sea bed. Gray-black coloring, lighter in the young. Reaches a width of 5 feet (1.5 meters). Found from New Jersey to Brazil.

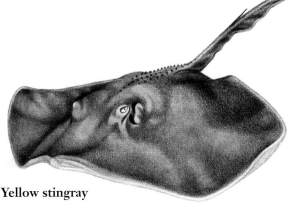

### Yellow stingray
*Urolophus jamaicensis*

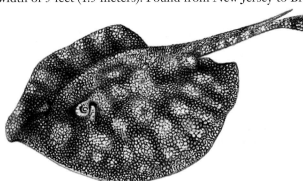

Disc-shaped body; rounded nose; rounded pectoral fin tips. The short tail has poisonous spines at the tip. Yellow-brown coloring with dark markings of varying size. Lives on sandy sea beds, where it buries itself close to the reefs. Can measure up to 30 inches (76 centimeters) in width. Found from North Carolina to Venezuela.

## MYLIOBATIDAE FAMILY

### Spotted eagle ray ▶
*Aetobatus narinari*

Lozenge-shaped body; big, pointed wings; pointed, convex head. The tail is almost 3 times as long as the body and has toothed spines along it. The back is dark in coloring with numerous light spots. Lives in deep reef channels close to shady beds. Grows up to 8 feet (2.5 meters) in width. Found in circumtropical waters.

## MURAENIDAE FAMILY

### Green moray
*Gymnothorax funebris*

◀ Easily identified by its green color, which varies in intensity from specimen to specimen, but is always uniform. Nocturnal; hides in reef crevices, often in shallow water, during the day. Can be easily approached, but may attack when provoked. Grows up to 7.5 feet (over 2 meters) in length. Found from Florida to Brazil.

### Spotted moray
*Gymnothorax moringa*

Common in shallow sea beds rich in vegetation, where it hides in crevices during the day, coming out at night to hunt. Yellow-white coloring with numerous brown or red-black markings. Can grow up to 5 feet (1.5 meters) in length. Found from South Carolina to Brazil.

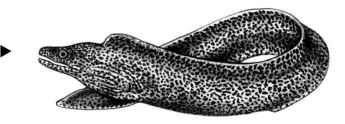

### Purplemouth moray
*Gymnothorax vicinus*

Identified by its yellow eyes, black-edged dorsal fin, and mouth, which is purple inside. Nocturnal; lives on rocky sea ◀ beds and along reefs, including shallow ones. Grows up to 5 feet (1.5 meters). Found from Florida to Brazil to the Canary Isles.

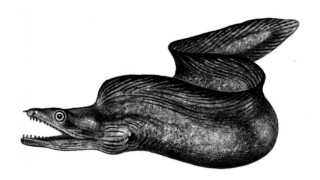

### Chain moray
*Echidna catenata*

Powerful body, tall and compressed at the back; short head; dorsal fin starts behind the bronchial opening. Yellow coloring with lighter chain-shaped pattern; yellow eyes. Prefers shallow, rocky coral sea beds with abundant crevices where it can hide. Grows up to 20 inches (50 centimeters) long. Found from Florida to Brazil.

## CONGRIDAE FAMILY

### Sand eel
*Heteroconger halis*

Elongated body; tapered head; large eyes; small mouth. Gray-brown coloring. Lives in colonies on sandy beds where it stays buried, leaving its mouth and part of its body outside. Grows up to 24 inches (60 centimeters) long. Found throughout the Caribbean.

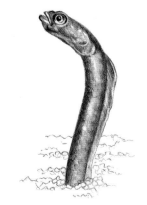

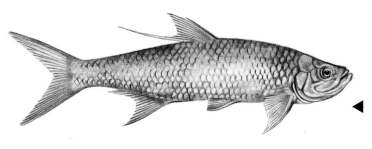

## ALBULIDAE FAMILY

### Bonefish
*Albula vulpes*

Tapered body; pointed nose; well-developed, downturned mouth. Last ray on dorsal and anal fins is filament-shaped. Tends to come into the coastal sandy beds with the tide. Found on coral sea beds with abundant sandy areas and reef channels. Grows over 3 feet (1 meter) long. Found from New Brunswick to Brazil.

## ANTENNARIDAE FAMILY

### Longlure frogfish
*Antennarius multiocellatus*

Deep, spherical body; stubby pelvic and pectoral fins; high dorsal fin with long filament for luring prey. Camouflaged to darken when frightened; motionless unless closely approached. Up to 5.5 inches (14 centimeters) long. Found from Florida to the Caribbean.

## MEGALOPIDAE FAMILY

### Tarpon
*Megalops atlanticus*

Big, robust body; oblique, upturned mouth. Silvery body covered in large scales. Last ray of dorsal fin long and threadlike. Lives in surface waters where there is very little light. Measures up to 8 feet (2.5 meters) long. Found from Virginia to Brazil.

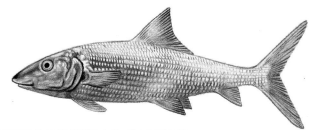

## SYNODONTIDAE FAMILY

### Lizardfish
*Synodus intermedius*

Robust, elongated body; flat underbelly; wide mouth with many small teeth. Dark blotch on the operculum and yellowish lengthwise stripes along the sides. Lives on sandy beds in which it buries itself. Grows up to 22 inches (55 centimeters) long. Found from North Carolina to Brazil.

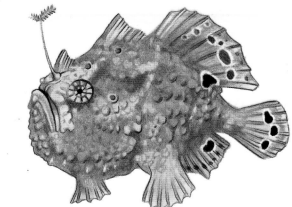

### Ocellated frogfish
*Antennarius ocellatus*

Very similar to longlure frogfish, distinguished from it by 3 ocellar marks: 1 lateral, 1 dorsal, and 1 caudal. Lives in rocky coral habitats and on sandy and muddy bottoms. Color varies from brownish red to brownish yellow. Measures up to 15 inches (38 centimeters) long. Found from North Carolina to the Caribbean.

## OGCOCEPHALIDAE FAMILY

### Spotted batfish
*Ogcocephalus radiatus*

Strangely shaped, like a flattened disc with stubby pectoral fins and a tail. Its back is covered with small dark spots. It likes both rocky and sandy beds, tending to bury itself in the latter. Measures up to 15 inches (38 centimeters) long. Found in Florida and in the Bahamas.

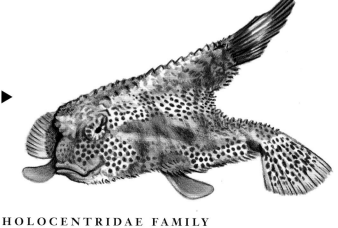

## HOLOCENTRIDAE FAMILY

### Longspine squirrelfish
*Holocentrus rufus*

Compressed, oval body; front of dorsal fin has robust white-tipped spiny rays. Hides in crevices during the day; at night hunts for mollusks, crustaceans, and echinoderms. Up to 11 inches (28 centimeters) long. Found from Bermuda to Venezuela.

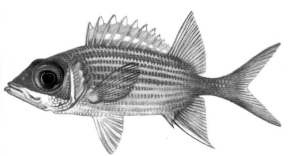

### Squirrelfish
*Holocentrus ascensionis*

Very similar to the longspine squirrelfish; distinguished mainly by its yellow-green dorsal fin. Stays in the darker areas of the reef in the daytime. Likes shallow coral sea beds with abundant crevices and small caves. Measures up to 14 inches (35 centimeters) long. Found from North Carolina to Brazil.

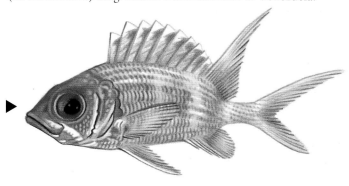

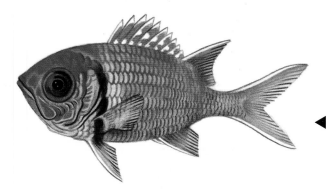

### Blackbar soldierfish
*Myripristis jacobus*

Oval-bodied; big head; large eyes. Red body with a black bar covering the rear edge of the opercula. Stays hidden in caves in the daytime; swims upside down because of the light that reflects off the sea bed. Measures up to 8 inches (20 centimeters) long. Found from Georgia to Brazil right to the Cape Verde Islands.

## AULOSTOMATIDAE FAMILY

### Trumpetfish
*Aulostomus maculatus*

Elongated body; tubular nose; terminal mouth with a thin barbel underneath its lower jaw. The dorsal fin consists of a series of separate spiny rays. Lives close to reefs where it camouflages itself by changing color and swimming in an almost vertical position. Timid and hard to approach. Can measure over 3 feet (1 meter) long. Found from Florida to Brazil.

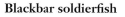

## FISTULARIDAE FAMILY

### Bluespotted cornetfish
*Fistularia tabacaria*

Elongated body; tubular nose; terminal mouth. Two central rays are elongated. Found near underwater meadows and reefs with sandy beds, alone or in small groups. Up to 6 feet (almost 2 meters) long. Found from Nova Scotia to Brazil.

## SYNGNATHIDAE FAMILY

### Lined seahorse
*Hippocampus erectus*

Unique body shape, made up of bony rings on which its head is set at an angle. Found in areas rich in vegetation, where it camouflages itself by anchoring to the algae with its prehensile tail. Grows up to 6.5 inches (17 centimeters) long. Found from Nova Scotia to Argentina.

## SCORPENIDI FAMILY

### Coral scorpionfish
*Scorpaena plumieri*

Powerful body; growths and appendages on nose. Greenish brown with red shading. Three dark vertical bars on the tail. The inside of the pectoral fins is dark with small white marks. This is one of the most common scorpionfish on coral reefs. Grows up to 16 inches (40 centimeters) long. Found from New York to Brazil.

## SERRANIDAE FAMILY

### Jewfish
*Epinephelus itajara*

One of the biggest Atlantic groupers. Wide, flat head. Greenish gray in color with small black marks. Usually makes its den in caves or wrecks. Grows up to 8 feet (2.5 meters) long. Its sheer size makes it potentially dangerous. Found from Florida to Brazil and in Africa from Senegal to Congo.

### Red grouper
*Epinephelus morio*

Sturdy, tapered body. The second spiny ray on the dorsal fin is bigger than the others. Concave caudal fin with pointed lobes in adult fish. Often stays immobile on the sea bed to camouflage itself. Measures up to 36 inches (90 centimeters) long. Found from Massachusetts to Brazil.

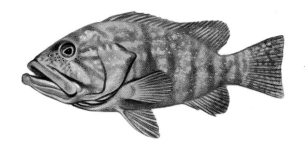

### Nassau grouper
*Ephinephelus striatus*

Tapered body; small pelvic fins. Common on coral sea beds, where it rarely strays from the area immediately surrounding its den. Changes color rapidly when frightened or curious. Shoals of thousands form in small areas for spawning. Grows over 3 feet (1 meter) long. Widespread from North Carolina to Brazil.

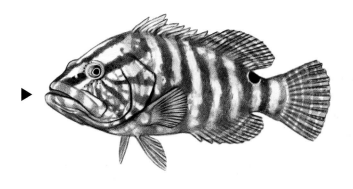

## Graysby
*Epinephelus cruentatus*

Grouper with a small, tapered body; rounded edge to its tail. Light-colored body with numerous reddish marks all over. Lives on coral beds from the surface to depths of 230 feet (70 meters). Grows up to 12 inches (30 centimeters) long. Found from Florida to Brazil.

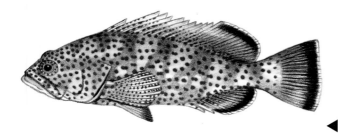

## Red hind
*Epinephelus guttatus*

One of the most common groupers in shallow coral sea beds; often seen resting immobile on the bottom. Light-colored body with reddish marks. Dorsal, anal, and caudal fins have black edges. Measures up to 24 inches (60 centimeters) long. Found from Florida to Brazil.

## Coney
*Epinephelus fulvus*

Tapered body; straight-edged or slightly rounded caudal fin with distinct corners. Coloring tends to differ with depth. Gregarious; prefers reefs abounding in crevices, from which it does not often stray. Allows divers to approach slowly. Grows up to 16 inches (40 centimeters) long. Found from Florida to Brazil.

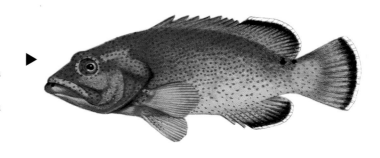

## Tiger grouper
*Mycteroperca tigris*

Tapered body; distinctive, light-colored vertical bars on its sides, which contribute to the tigerish looks. Background color tends to red. Young fish are yellow. Lives in sheltered parts of the reef. Measures up to 33 inches (85 centimeters) long. Found from Florida to Brazil.

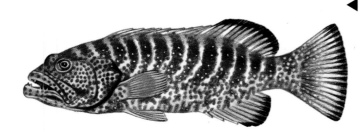

## Black grouper
*Mycteroperca bonaci*

Long body; distinctive rounded edge to dorsal and anal fins. Color varies from red-brown to black, with patches that vary in intensity. The dorsal, anal, and tail fins are edged in black. Lives on the reef, often moving into the open sea nearby. Measures up to 3.5 feet (over 1 meter) long. Found from Massachusetts to Brazil.

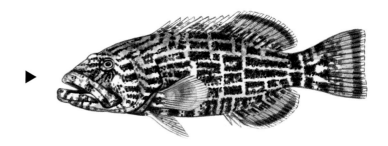

## Sand perch
*Diplectrum formosum*

Small, elongated, slightly compressed body. Pre-operculum has two groups of diverging spines. Light-colored with blue horizontal stripes on its head and sides. Lives in meadowlands or coral, where it digs dens for itself. Measures up to 10 inches (25 centimeters) long. Found from North Carolina to Uruguay.

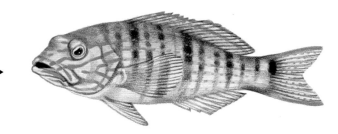

## Greater soapfish
*Rypticus saponaceus*

Pointed front profile; flattened on the back of the head. Dorsal fin set back with a rounded rear edge. Lives in shallow water close to reefs and on sandy beds. If startled, secretes a mucus poisonous to other fish. Measures up to 13 inches (33 centimeters) long. Found from Florida to Brazil and in the eastern Atlantic.

## Butter hamlet
*Hypoplectrus unicolor*

Deep, compressed body. Lower edge of the pre-operculum finely toothed. Distinct, saddle-shaped mark on caudal peduncle. Prefers coral reefs, where it swims close to the sea bed. Measures up to 5 inches (13 centimeters) long. Found from Florida to Brazil.

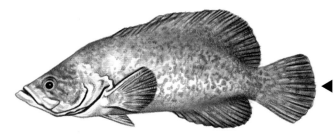

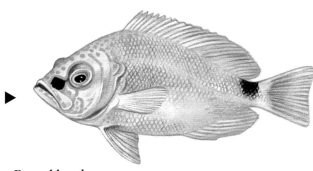

## Barred hamlet
*Hypoplectrus puella*

Compressed body; slightly pointed snout. Brown-yellow with a dark triangular blotch in the center of each flank. Prefers rocky, shallow waters and coral reefs up to depths of 75 feet (23 meters). Can be approached, but is quick to flee into crevices for shelter. Measures up to 5 inches (13 centimeters) long. Found from Florida to the Caribbean.

## Indigo hamlet
*Hypoplectrus indigo*

Similar to barred hamlet, but distinguished by its bluish color with vertical white bars. Prefers coral sea beds, where it swims close to the bottom. Can be approached slowly. Measures up to 5 inches (13 centimeters) long. Found from Florida to the Caymans to Belize.

## Tobaccofish
*Serranus tabacarius*

Tapered body; broad horizontal stripe of brownish orange. Lives close to the sea bed on the border between reefs and sandy beds or in areas strewn with reef detritus. Tends to become gregarious at depths greater than 165 feet (50 meters). Measures up to 7 inches (18 centimeters) long. Found from Florida to Brazil.

## Tigerfish
*Serranus tigrinus*

Small, elongated, compressed body; pointed snout. Opercula spiny with toothed edges. Marked with dark vertical bars. Tips of caudal lobes yellowish. Lives on coral sea beds or meadowlands. Measures up to 6 inches (15 centimeters) long. Common in the Caribbean.

## Peppermint bass
*Liopropoma rubre*

Small, tapered body; double dorsal fin. Tip of dorsal, anal, and tail fins are the same color. Flanks have red stripes. Tends to stay hidden in crevices and hollows and is not often seen, although it is common. Measures over 3 inches (8 centimeters) long. Found from Florida to Venezuela.

## GRAMMATIDAE FAMILY

### Fairy basslet
*Gramma loreto*

Small with highly characteristic coloring: half purple, half yellow. Lives in small schools in hollows and crevices, where it swims upside down because of the reflected light. Measures over 3 inches (8 centimeters) long. Found from Bermuda to Venezuela.

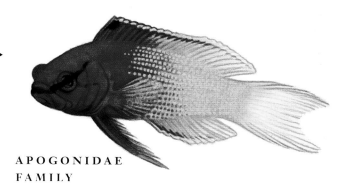

## APOGONIDAE FAMILY

### Spotted cardinalfish
*Apogon maculatus*

Small, robust, oval body; deep caudal peduncle. Red with a spot on the operculum and at base of second dorsal fin. Prefers surface water caves during the day. Measures over 5 inches (13 centimeters) long. Found from Florida to the Gulf of Mexico.

## CIRRHITIDAE FAMILY

### Redspotted hawkfish
*Amblycirrhitus pinos*

Small, deep body; pointed nose. Spiny rays of dorsal fin have fringed points. Distinctive red spots on nose, back, and dorsal fin. Lives on reefs, where it waits in ambush on the sea bed. Measures over 4 inches (11 centimeters) long. Found from Florida to the Gulf of Mexico.

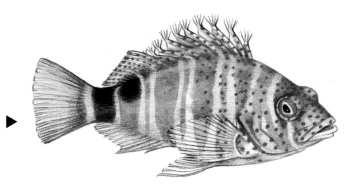

## PRIACANTHIDAE FAMILY

### Glasseye snapper
*Heteropriacanthus cruentatus*

Robust, compressed body; square head; oblique mouth angled upward; very large eyes. Reddish with silvery bars that disappear on the back. Prefers surface waters, where it inhabits the less illuminated areas during the day. Measures up to 12 inches (30 centimeters) long. Found in circumtropical waters.

## MALACANTHIDAE FAMILY

### Sand tilefish
*Malacanthus plumieri*

Elongated body; very large lips; crescent-shaped tail with
pointed lobes. Yellowish blue with yellow and blue stripes on
the head. Tail is often yellow. Lives on sandy and rubble-
strewn sea beds, where it digs a den. Measures up to 24 inches
(60 centimeters) long. Found from North Carolina to Brazil.

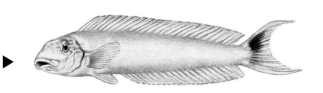

## CENTROPOMIDAE FAMILY

### Snook
*Centropomus undecimalis*

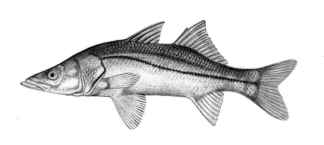

Robust body; pointed head; dorsal fin has a sharply angled
profile. The lateral line is dark and continues to the rear edge
of the tail. Lives in mangrove-filled coastal waters. Measures
over 4 feet (over 1 meter) long. Found from South Carolina
to Brazil.

## CARANGIDAE FAMILY

### Crevalle jack
*Caranx hippos*

Deep, elongated body, very tapered and convex at the front.
Thin, characteristically forked, tail. Young are gregarious and
more common in coastal waters; adults tend to be solitary,
more common in open water and along the outer edge of the
reef. Measures over 3 feet (1 meter) long. Found from Nova
Scotia to Uruguay and in the eastern Atlantic.

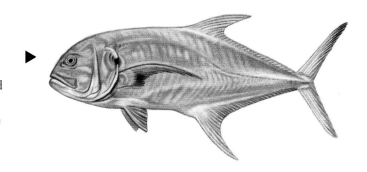

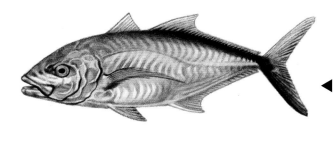

### Bar jack
*Carangoides ruber*

Elongated, tapering, silvery body, marked at the base of the
dorsal fin by a dark band that stretches to the lower caudal
lobe. Lives in shoals of varying size and often follows shoals of
mullet and stingray to feed on invertebrates they uncover.
Measures up to 24 inches (60 centimeters) long. Found from
New Jersey to Venezuela.

### Rainbow fish
*Elagatic bipinnulata*

Elongated, spindle-shaped body with 2 light blue horizontal
stripes separated by a green or yellowish streak. Common in
open water; often moves in close to the outer slopes of the reef.
Lives in shoals and seems to be attracted by the air bubbles
produced by scuba-diving equipment. Measures up to 4 feet
(over 1 meter) long. Found in all circumtropical waters.

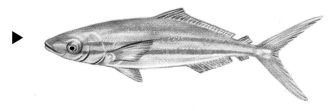

## Horse-eye jack
*Caranx latus*

Relatively deep, compressed body. Its yellow tail distinguishes it from the other carangids. Lives in shoals in open water above the deepest reefs, often mixing with other carangids. Measures up to 28 inches (70 centimeters) long. Found from New Jersey to Brazil.

▶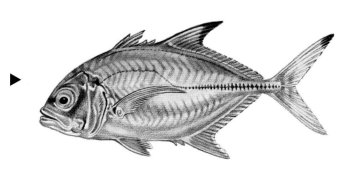

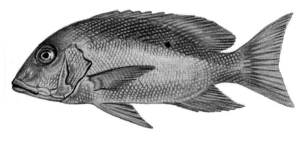

## Palometa
*Trachinotus goodei*

Lozenge-shaped body, distinguished by large rays on the dorsal and anal fins. Silver color with 3 to 5 vertical black streaks. Lives in coastal waters among coral formations. Measures up to 20 inches (50 centimeters) long. Found from Massachusetts to Argentina.

◀

### LUTJANIDAE FAMILY

## Yellowtail snapper
*Ocyurus chrysurus*

▶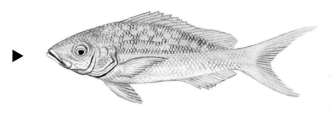

Elongated body; pronounced forked tail with pointed lobes. Purple-blue color with horizontal yellow stripe and small spots. Swims alone or in small groups close to reef or meadowlands. More active at night. Measures up to 30 inches (75 centimeters) long. Found from Massachusetts to Brazil.

## Mutton snapper
*Lutjanus analis*

◀ Robust, deep body; olive colored with blackish streaks that are more marked in fish under 16 inches (40 centimeters) long. Adults prefer rocky and coral sea beds; young found more often on sandy beds and in meadowlands. Measures up to 30 inches (75 centimeters) long. Found from Massachusetts to Brazil.

## Cubera snapper
*Lutjanus cyanopterus*

Tapered, robust body; large lips. Gray with red reflections at the front. Prefers rather deep rock or coral sea beds. Young are more common along the shoreline. Measures over 5 feet (1.5 meters) long. Found from New Jersey to Brazil.

▶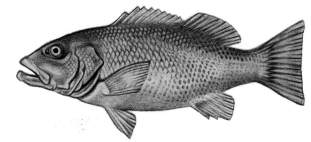

## HAEMULIDAE FAMILY

### Porkfish
*Anisotremus virginicus*

Compressed body, very deep at the front. Two characteristic dark vertical bars on the head and a series of blue and yellow horizontal streaks. Swims alone or in small groups, more common above the reef during the day. Young act as cleaner fish. Measures up to 16 inches (40 centimeters) long. Found from Florida to Brazil.

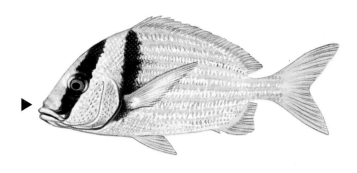

### Bluestriped grunt
*Haemulon sciurus*

Deep, compressed body, with dark-colored rear part, including the dorsal and tail fins. Background color is yellow with numerous blue horizontal stripes. Forms large shoals near the coast on rocky or sandy beds. Measures up to 18 inches (45 centimeters) long. Found from South Carolina to Brazil.

### French grunt
*Haemulon flavolineatum*

Deep body; pointed snout; small mouth. Yellowish with numerous blue streaks, horizontal above the lateral line and oblique below. Prefers coral sea beds, where it forms shoals of up to 1,000 fish. Likes poorly illuminated areas. Measures up to 12 inches (30 centimeters) long. Found from South Carolina to Brazil.

## SPARIDAE FAMILY

### Saucereye porgy
*Calamus calamus*

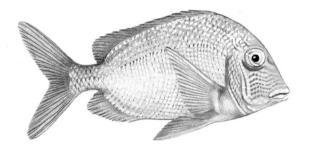

Compressed body, deep at the front; blunt nose. Blue-gray coloring with rounded blue blotch between the eyes and yellow corners to the mouth. Lives close to the sandy beds in the reefs. Measures up to 16 inches (40 centimeters) long. Found from North Carolina to Brazil.

## SCIAENIDAE FAMILY

### Reef croaker
*Odontoscion dentex*

Elongated, compressed body; big, oblique, terminal mouth. Reddish body with a black blotch at the base of the pelvic fin. Prefers rocky habitats and shallow coral reefs, tending to stay in poorly lit areas. Measures up to 10 inches (25 centimeters) long. Found from Florida to Brazil.

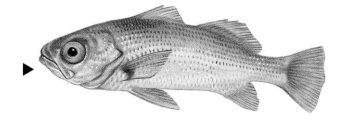

## Jack-knife fish
*Equetus lanceolatus*

Body deep in front and very pointed in rear. Characteristically deep forward dorsal fin, especially in the young. Dark bar runs from the tip of the dorsal fin to the tail. Prefers the darker parts of reefs and hollows. Measures up to 10 inches (25 centimeters) long. Found from South Carolina to Brazil.

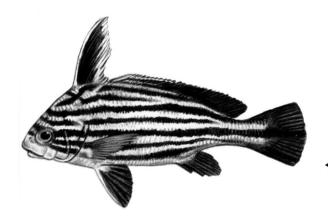

## High hat
*Pareques acuminatus*

Deep body in front; less deep in rear part; stumpy; well-defined dorsal fin. Red-brown with longitudinal whitish stripes. Prefers surface waters close to rocky and coral bottoms, near caves and poorly illuminated areas. Measures up to 9 inches (23 centimeters) long. Found from South Carolina to Brazil.

### MULLIDAE FAMILY

## Yellow goatfish
*Mulloidichthys martinicus*

Tapered body; snout has a slightly convex and pointed edge. Olive-colored back with light-colored flanks; horizontal yellow bar stretching to the tail. Forms small shoals on the sandy beds close to reefs. Measures up to 16 inches (40 centimeters) long. Found from the Caribbean to the Cape Verde Islands.

## Spotted goatfish
*Pseudopeneus maculatus*

Tapered body; slightly pointed snout. Edge of operculum has a spine, quite pronounced in some cases. Three large blackish blotches on the sides of the body. Forms small groups of 4 to 5 to hunt. Grows over 10 inches (26 centimeters) long. Found from Florida to Brazil.

### PEMPHERIDAE FAMILY

## Glassfish
*Pempheris schomburgki*

Small, compressed, oval body; tapered at the rear. Silvery pink color, with long black-edged anal fin. Lives in shoals in grottoes or reef crevices, coming out at night. Measures up to 6 inches (16 centimeters) long. Found from Florida to Brazil.

### KIPHOSIDAE FAMILY

## Bermuda chub
*Kyphosus sectatrix*

Deep, oval body; small terminal mouth. Gray with thin bronze horizontal stripes. Forms shoals close to coral and rocky sea beds rich in algae. Up to 30 inches (76 centimeters) long. Found from Massachusetts to Brazil.

## EPHIPPIDAE FAMILY

### Atlantic spadefish
*Chaetodipterus faber*

Very deep, compressed body; lobes of dorsal and anal fins very elongated at the rear. Grayish with 4 to 5 dark vertical bands. Forms small schools that swim in open water away from the reef. Sometimes spontaneously approaches divers. Grows up to 36 inches (90 centimeters) long. Found from Massachusetts to Brazil.

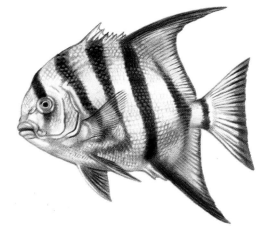

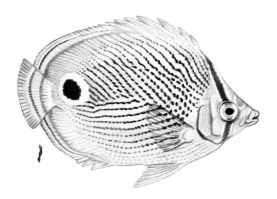

### Reef butterflyfish
*Chaetodon sedentarius*

Deep, compressed body; almost vertical rear profile. Yellowish coloring with a dark, wide band at the rear, running from dorsal to anal fin. Prefers coral bottoms where it goes as deep as 295 feet (90 meters). Measures up to 6 inches (15 centimeters) long. Found from North Carolina to Brazil.

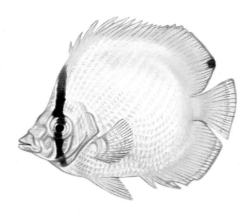

### Longsnout butterflyfish
*Chaetodon aculeatus*

Compressed, very deep body; well-developed spiny rays on dorsal fin; long, pointed snout. Solitary; prefers the deepest coral sea beds and reef crevices, where it takes shelter when frightened. Measures up to 4 inches (10 centimeters) long. Found from Florida to Venezuela.

## CHAETODONTIDAE FAMILY

### Foureye butterflyfish
*Chaetodon capistratus*

Deep, compressed body; yellow fins with small black spot on rear edge of the dorsal fin. Tends to become dark at night. Usually swims in pairs close to reefs and rocky sea beds. Grows up to 8 inches (20 centimeters) long. Found from Massachusetts to Brazil.

### Spotfin butterflyfish
*Chaetodon ocellatus*

Deep, compressed body; yellow fins; small black mark on rear edge of dorsal fin. Tends to turn a darker color at night. Generally swims in pairs close to reefs and rocky bottoms. Grows up to 8 inches (20 centimeters) long. Found from Massachusetts to Brazil.

## Banded butterflyfish
*Chaetodon striatus*

Deep, compressed body; whitish coloring with 3 dark slanting bars, the first of which covers the eye. Young fish have an ocellar marking on the caudal peduncle. Lives alone or in pairs, close to coral. Measures up to 6 inches (16 centimeters) long. Found from Massachusetts to Brazil.

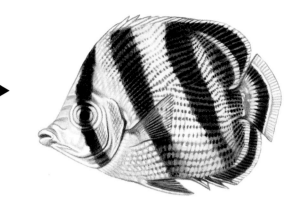

## POMACANTHIDAE FAMILY

### Gray angelfish
*Pomacanthus arcuatus*

Deep, compressed body; dorsal and caudal lobes pointed at rear; tail fin has a straight trailing edge. Gray-brown coloring, with a very pale mouth. Lives alone or in pairs in the richest areas of the reef. Measures up to 20 inches (50 centimeters) long. Found from Bermuda to Brazil.

## French angelfish
*Pomacanthus paru*

Rounded, compressed body; rear lobes of dorsal and anal fins very pointed. Blackish coloring with yellow markings on snout and pectoral fins. Prefers the reef closest to the surface and richest in gorgonians. Measures up to 12 inches (30 centimeters) long. Found from Florida to Brazil.

### Rock beauty
*Holacanthus tricolor*

Distinctive colors: yellow front body and tail sections, black central section, and blue mouth. Pointed lobes to dorsal, anal, and caudal fins. Extremely territorial; stays close to its own area of the reef. Measures up to 8 inches (20 centimeters) long. Found from Georgia to Brazil.

## Blue angelfish
*Holocanthus bermudensis*

Deep, compressed body; rear lobes of dorsal and anal fins very pointed, extending past the trailing edge of the caudal fin. Blue with yellow-edged fins. Prefers the reef closest to the surface. Measures up to 15 inches (38 centimeters) long. Found from Florida to Yucatan.

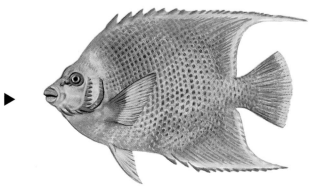

## Queen angelfish
*Holacanthus ciliaris*

Deep, compressed body; rear lobes of dorsal and anal fins very pointed, extending past the trailing caudal fin. Yellow, densely spotted with blue on the sides and a blue blotch on the head. Lives on the reef closest to the surface and also in the deepest parts at over 165 feet (50 meters). Measures up to 18 inches (45 centimeters) long. Found from Bermuda to Brazil.

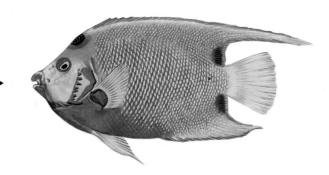

## POMACENTRIDAE FAMILY

## Blue chromis
*Chromis cyanea*

Small, oval body; deeply cleft tail fin. Bluish with black-edged caudal lobes. Quite common around the reef, where it forms shoals. Measures up to 5 inches (13 centimeters) long. Found from Florida to Venezuela.

## Cherubfish
*Centropyge argi*

Small, oval body. Yellow markings on head and part of the back; blue sides, belly, and tail. Prefers the deepest parts of the coral bed, usually over 98 feet (30 meters), where it sometimes forms small groups. Measures up to 3 inches (8 centimeters) long. Found from Bermuda to Venezuela.

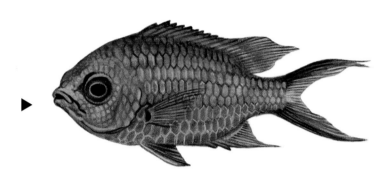

## Brown chromis
*Chromis multilineata*

Swarthy, gray fish with a black spot at the base of the pectoral fins and yellow tips to the dorsal fin and caudal lobes. Lives in groups above coral formations. Measures up to 6.5 inches (17 centimeters) long. Found from Florida to Brazil.

## Beaugregory
*Stegastes leucostictos*

Small, slightly oval in shape; forked tail with rounded lobes. Brownish coloring with a light yellow tail. Territorial; prefers sandy sea beds rich in algae and detritus. Measures up to 4 inches (10 centimeters) long. Found from Maine to Brazil.

## Bicolor damselfish
*Stegastes partitus*

Small, compressed, oval body; small terminal mouth. Dark front section; white at the back. Lives close to the higher parts of the reef, where it defends its territory from other fishes of the same species. Measures up to 5 inches (12 centimeters) long. Found from Florida to the Gulf of Mexico.

## Three-spot damselfish
*Stegastes planifrons*

Small, compressed, oval body; small terminal mouth. Dark coloring with yellow-rimmed eyes and black spots at the base of pectoral fins and caudal peduncle. Lives in the reef closest to the surface, rich in algae, where it establishes its own territory and defends it tenaciously. Measures up to 5 inches (12 centimeters) long. Found from Florida to the Gulf of Mexico.

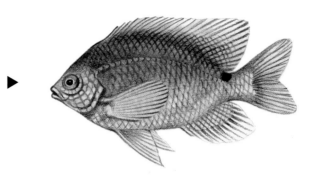

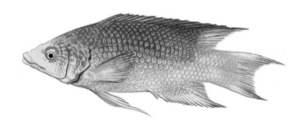

## Sergeant major
*Abudefduf saxatilis*

Compressed, ovoid, deep body; covered with rough scales, which extend to the fins. Silvery white with dark vertical bars and a yellow stripe at the base of the dorsal fin. Lives in shoals in the reef closest to the surface. Measures up to 8 inches (20 centimeters) long. Found from Rhode Island to Uruguay.

## Yellowtail damselfish
*Microspatodon chrysurus*

Small, robust body. Brownish coloring with small blue markings and distinctive yellow tail. The young tend to stay among the branches of fire corals, sometimes acting as cleaner fish. Adults occupy small territories in the reef closest to the surface. Measures up to 8 inches (20 centimeters) long. Found from Florida to Venezuela.

## LABRIDAE FAMILY

## Spanish hogfish
*Bodianus rufus*

Robust body; pointed head. Purple back; rest of the body yellowish. Swims continuously close to the sea bed, showing no fear at all, not even of divers. Measures up to 16 inches (40 centimeters) long. Found from Florida to Brazil.

## Spotfin hogfish
*Bodianus pulchellus*

Robust body; pointed snout; pointed rear lobes on dorsal and anal fins. Adults are red with yellow tail and partially yellow caudal fin. Common on coral reefs over 65 feet (20 meters) deep. Measures up to 8 inches (20 centimeters) long. Found from Florida to Brazil.

### Hogfish
*Lachnolaimus maximus*

Fairly large; pointed head. Identified by the very well developed first rays of dorsal fin. Whitish coloring with a dark bar stretching along the back from mouth to tail. Prefers sandy sea beds, where it likes to dig for its prey. Measures up to 35 inches (90 centimeters) long. Found from North Carolina to Brazil.

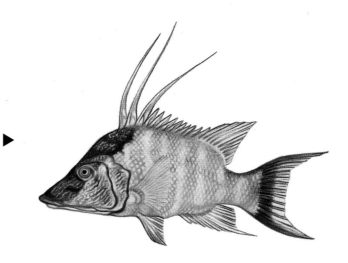

### Bluehead wrasse
*Thalassoma bifasciatum*

Elongated, compressed body. Coloring varies greatly according to age. Adults are greenish at the rear and bluish at the front with black and white stripes in between. The young are yellowish. Found in a great number of different habitats. Measures up to 7 inches (18 centimeters) long. Found from Florida to Venezuela.

### Puddingwife
*Halichoeres radiatus*

Very deep body. Blue-green coloring with yellow-edged caudal fin. Uncommon and hard to approach: swims continuously and is very suspicious. Measures up to 20 inches (50 centimeters) long. Found from North Carolina to Brazil.

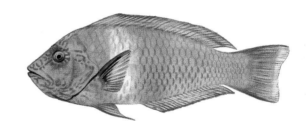

### Slippery dick
*Halichoeres bivittatus*

Deep, tapered body; large caudal fin. Extremely variable coloring, mainly greenish with a horizontal dark band along the sides. Lobes of caudal fin have dark tips. Found in various different habitats, from coral reefs to sandy sea beds to underwater meadows. Measures up to 10 inches (26 centimeters) long. Found from North Carolina to Brazil.

### Creole wrasse
*Clepticus parrae*

Large, tapered body; pointed lobes of dorsal and anal fins; slightly lunar-shaped tail. Adults are dark purple with a yellowish rear part and a pale mouth. Prefers the deepest parts of the reef, where it forms large shoals before sunset. Measures up to 12 inches (30 centimeters) long. Found from North Carolina to the Gulf of Mexico.

# SCARIDAE FAMILY

## Blue parrotfish
*Scarus coeruleus*

Tapered, robust body. Adult males have a characteristic frontal bump that modifies the front profile of the snout. Mainly blue in color. Feeds principally on algae and for this reason it moves swiftly from one part of the reef to another. Measures up to 35 inches (90 centimeters) long. Found from Maryland to Brazil.

## Queen parrotfish
*Scarus vetula*

Blue-green with scales edged in pink-orange. Nose has broad blue stripes around the mouth and close to the eyes. Lives on coral reefs up to 82 feet (25 meters) deep. Measures up to 24 inches (60 centimeters) long. Found from Florida to Argentina.

## Spotlight parrotfish
*Sparisoma viride*

Mainly green coloring; yellow-orange slanting bars on head; caudal fin and a yellow mark on the operculum. Reasonably common where coral sea beds alternate with areas rich in algae. Measures up to 20 inches (50 centimeters) long. Found from Florida to Brazil.

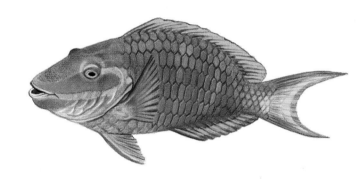

## Red-banded parrotfish
*Sparisoma aurofrenatum*

Green coloring with red and orange shading; orange bar at each side of the mouth; fins shaded with purple. Prefers reefs where there is an abundance of algae. Measures up to 14 inches (35 centimeters) long. Found from Florida to Brazil.

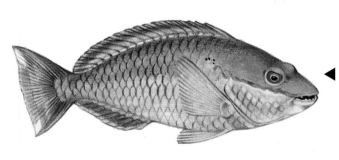

# OPISTOGNATHIDAE FAMILY

## Yellowhead jawfish
*Opistognathus aurifrons*

Small, elongated, tapered body; short, powerful head; large eyes. Blue coloring with a yellowish head. Bottom-dweller that lives close to a den it digs itself. Measures up to 4 inches (10 centimeters) long. Found from Florida to Venezuela.

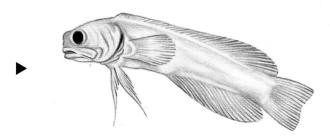

## SPHYRAENIDAE FAMILY

### Great barracuda
*Sphyraena barracuda*

Tapered, subcylindrical body; long, pointed snout; prominent lower jaw; 2 clearly separated dorsal fins; caudal fin slightly lunar-shaped, with pointed lobes. Coloring is silvery with dark vertical bands and small spots near the caudal fin. Lives in coastal waters above coral, sandy, or meadowland sea beds. Measures up to 6.5 feet (2 meters) long. Found in all circumtropical waters.

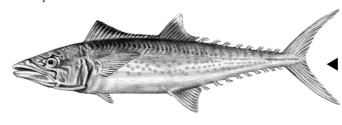

## SCOMBRIDAE FAMILY

### Cero
*Scomberomorus regalis*

Very tapered body; caudal peduncle has numerous small dorsal and pelvic fins; distinctive forked tail. Silver body with a series of dark blotches surrounding a gold horizontal stripe. Lives in open waters along the outer slopes of the reef. Measures up to 4 feet (over 1 meter). Found from Massachusetts to Brazil.

## BLENNIDAE FAMILY

### Red-mouthed blenny
*Ophioblennius atlanticus*

Compressed body; blunt nose; distinctive big lips. Dark with yellow or pink shading on the pectoral and caudal fins. Territorial; prefers rocky sea beds and the parts of the reef closest to the surface. Measures up to 5 inches (13 centimeters) long. Found from North Carolina to Brazil.

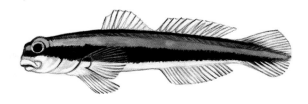

## GOBIDAE FAMILY

### Neon goby
*Gobiosoma oceanops*

Small cleaner fish, which forms groups with others of its species in characteristic "service stations." Easily identified by its dark coloring, on which 2 blue fluorescent horizontal stripes stand out. Measures up to 2 inches (5 centimeters) long. Found from Florida to Honduras.

### Cleaner goby
*Gobiosoma genie*

Small cleaner fish, which forms shoals in particular areas of the reef. Dark back and pale underside, with black streaks and a yellow V-shaped mark between the eyes. Measures up to 1.5 inches (4 centimeters) long. Found in the Caribbean.

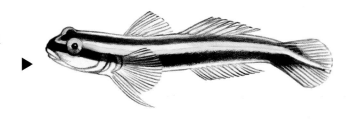

## ACANTHURIDAE FAMILY

### Surgeonfish
*Acanthurus chirurgus*

Deep, compressed body. Distinctive set of dark vertical bars, more or less visible. Usually lives alone or with other surgeonfish close to the reef. Measures up to 10 inches (25 centimeters) long. Found from Massachusetts to Brazil.

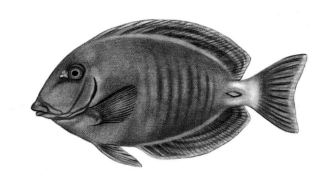

### Blue tang
*Acanthurus coeruleus*

Similar to surgeonfish but has no vertical bars. Color can vary from powder blue to deep purple. Measures up to 12 inches (30 centimeters) long. Found from Massachusetts to Brazil.

### Bahia surgeonfish
*Acanthurus bahianus*

Coloring varies from blue-gray to dark brown with light-colored spokes around the eyes. Prefers flat or slightly sloping coral sea beds. Measures up to 14 inches (35 centimeters) long. Found from Massachusetts to Brazil.

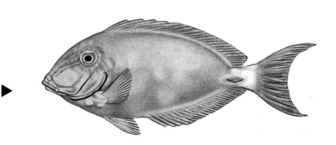

## BOTHIDAE FAMILY

### Ocellated turbot
*Bothus lunatus*

Identified by the series of ocellar spots on the body and the small bluish marks on the fins. Very elongated pelvic fin that is usually erect. Lives on sandy sea beds covered in detritus, where it camouflages itself. Measures up to 16 inches (40 centimeters) long. Found from Florida to Brazil.

## BALISTIDI FAMILY

### Gray triggerfish
*Balistes capriscus*

Has small bluish spots on the back and fins. Lives alone or in small groups near rocky sea beds rich in vegetation. Particularly fond of sea urchins as food. Measures up to 12 inches (30 centimeters) long. Found from Nova Scotia to Argentina.

### Queen triggerfish
*Balistes vetula*

Has streaming tips on dorsal and tail fins, 2 blue stripes on face, and distinctive small lines radiating from eye. Measures up to 24 inches (60 centimeters). Found in circumtropical seas.

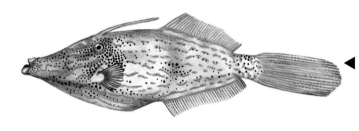

### Black durgon
*Melichthys niger*

Blue-black body with blue stripes at the base of dorsal and anal fins. Lives in small groups along the outer reef wall at depths of up to 196 feet (60 meters). Measures up to 20 inches (50 centimeters) long. Found in circumtropical seas.

### Sargasso triggerfish
*Xanthichthys ringens*

Compressed, oval body. Bright blue with 3 opercular black streaks and a number of dark, horizontal bands made up of small markings. Prefers the deepest parts of the reef. The young often live among sargasso (floating vegetation). Measures up to 10 inches (25 centimeters) long. Found from North Carolina to Brazil.

MONACANTHIDAE FAMILY

### Scrawled filefish
*Aluteres scriptus*

Tapered body; pointed snout; broad tail. Coloring characterized by irregular streaks and small blue markings. Solitary; lives in lagoons and along the outer reef wall, from which it heads for the open sea. Measures up to 3.5 feet (over 1 meter) long. Common in circumtropical seas.

OSTRACIIDAE FAMILY

### Smooth trunkfish
*Lactrophrys triqueter*

Triangular silhouette; large hexagonal bony scales. Dark coloring with numerous lighter marks. Usually solitary; sometimes forms small groups. Prefers coral sea beds but can be found on sandy beds. Measures up to 12 inches (30 centimeters) long. Found from Massachusetts to Brazil.

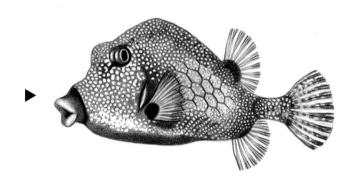

## Variegated trunkfish
*Lactophrys quadricornis*

Triangular silhouette; large caudal peduncle. Yellowish coloring with numerous blue streaks and marks. Usually solitary; prefers coral sea beds and meadowlands, where it camouflages itself. Measures up to 15 inches (38 centimeters) long. Found from Massachusetts to Brazil.

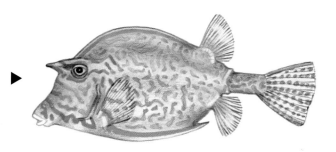

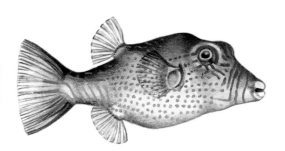

## TETRAODONTIDAE FAMILY

### Longnose pufferfish
*Canthigaster rostrata*

Small; very pointed nose; small terminal mouth. Dark coloring on the back and yellowish along the sides; blue streaks and marks around the eyes, close to the mouth and on the tail. Prefers coral sea beds and meadowlands. Measures over 4 inches (11 centimeters) long. Found from Florida to Brazil.

## Bandtail pufferfish
*Sphoeroides spengleri*

Elongated body, rounded at the front; large nostrils. Horizontal series of marks along the sides below the lateral line. Nearly always swims close to the sea bed, whether meadowlands, coral, or sandy and strewn with detritus. Measures up to 7 inches (18 centimeters) long. Found from Massachusetts to Brazil.

### Chequered pufferfish
*Sphoeroides testudineus*

Round, spindle-shaped body; light geometrical lines form a grid. Prefers coastal bays, rocks, and meadowlands. Not often found close to reefs. Measures up to 12 inches (30 centimeters) long. Found from Bermuda to Brazil.

## DIODONTIDE

### Burrfish
*Diodon hystrix*

Tapered body with a large, rounded front end; goggle eyes; mouth has a single dental plate in each jaw; skin covered in spines that become erect when the animal puffs up. Tends to stay in caves or other poorly illuminated areas of the reef during the day. Measures up to 35 inches (90 centimeters) long. Found in all circumtropical waters.

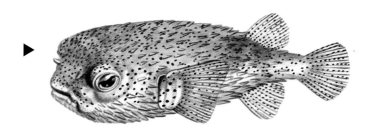

*Below:*
*A group of Atlantic spotted dolphins swims close to the sandy sea bed at Bahama Bank.*

*Front cover:*
*This picture shows the rich Caribbean sea bed where corals, gorgonians and sponges compete for living space.*

*Back cover (top):*
*A grey angelfish (Pomacanthus arcuatus) seems to observe the photographer with curiosity.*

*Back cover (bottom):*
*Two divers explore the Black Caves of Honduras.*

*Kurt Amsler wishes to thank his wife, Isabelle Amsler, Christopher J. Allison, Renate Bernd, Joe M. Clark, John Englander, Chris Ery, Cathy Church, Rebecca Fitzgerald, Roger Fivat, Stephen Frink, Maurits Groen, Doris Hagenbucher, Bill Horn, Jacques Imbert, Ben Rose, Marco Rosenfelder, Ron Reed, Kenneth G. Thompson, Divemaster Kevin, Charles Novalez, Captain Wesley, Frank Wirth, Aqua Safari, the crew of the* Seafever, Ocean Touren, Ocean Divers, *the crew of the* Rembrandt van Rijn, *and* UNEXSO.